39.95

D0706585

AN INTRODUCTION TO
BRADLEY'S METAPHYSICS

An Introduction to Bradley's Metaphysics

W. J. MANDER

CLARENDON PRESS · OXFORD
1994

Oxford University Press, Walton Street, Oxford OX2 6DP
Oxford New York Toronto
Delhi Bombay Calcutta Madras Karachi
Kuala Lumpur Singapore Hong Kong Tokyo
Nairobi Dar es Salaam Cape Town
Melbourne Auckland Madrid
and associated companies in
Berlin Ibadan

Oxford is a trade mark of Oxford University Press

Published in the United States
by Oxford University Press Inc., New York

© W. J. Mander 1994

British Library Cataloguing in Publication Data
Data available

Library of Congress Cataloging in Publication Data
Mander, W. J.
An introduction to Bradley's metaphysics / W. J. Mander.
Includes bibliographical references and index.
1. Bradley, F. H. (Francis Herbert), 1846–1924—Contributions in
metaphysics. 2. Metaphysics. I. Title.
B1618.B74M36 1994 110—dc20 93-37870
ISBN 0-19-824090-2

1 3 5 7 9 10 8 6 4 2

Typeset by Graphicraft Typesetters Ltd., Hong Kong
Printed in Great Britain
on acid-free paper by
Bookcraft (Bath) Ltd.
Midsomer Norton, Avon

PREFACE

PHILOSOPHICAL reputations wax and wane as each new generation considers the problems of philosophy afresh, and rewrites its history in the light of how it sees matters. Though perhaps inevitable, this dynamic, which in other aspects of life goes under the name of fashion, rarely makes for good criticism. Distortions and misunderstandings occur, as thinkers are squeezed into preconceived categories dictated by a certain world-view, rather than being allowed to stand in their own right as individuals, often with complex and multiple allegiances, who resist capture under any one simple label.

Few philosophers have experienced such rapid and radically changing fortunes as F. H. Bradley. In his heyday Bradley was held by many to be perhaps the greatest living philosopher in Britain. For instance, his book *Appearance and Reality* was described by Stout, the long-time editor of *Mind*, as having accomplished as much as is humanly possible in ontology.[1] Yet this high esteem among his supporters produced little by the way of serious critical commentary on his work. Nor was opinion on his philosophy undivided. From the beginning of the twentieth century there existed a small but rapidly growing group of philosophers, led initially by Russell and Moore, who were wholly opposed to Bradley in both philosophical temperament and opinion. It was this school that eventually came to dominate the philosophical scene, with the result that, by the middle of the century, Bradley's popularity had waned and his philosophy was almost universally rejected. Yet this did not make for better criticism, for much of this opposition largely failed to make contact with his real views, attacking but an imaginary or caricatured figure. None the less his detractors won the day, and since then Bradley's thought has been by and large neglected.

This is a great shame. For, while his views are more defensible than is commonly believed, and of great intrinsic interest, they are largely either unknown or known only in a highly distorted and

---

[1] According to Russell (1927), 38.

inaccurate form. Moreover, they connect interestingly with many ideas and themes which are current today. Fortunately, in recent years there has been once again a small, but growing, interest in his philosophy. While this has already reached several aspects of his work, his metaphysics have not yet received much renewed attention. This book aims to fill that gap. It begins with an introductory chapter and then works progressively through the basic elements of his system.

Before we can embark on any such exegetical or critical study, a question necessarily arises about the integrity of the Bradleian corpus. It is sometimes said that over his fifty-year-long career he considerably changed his opinions on a number of crucial issues.[2] Assessment of this claim is greatly complicated by the fact that his views about any one subject are rarely all found in a single place (for instance, his two major discussions of relations are separated by nearly thirty years). While not wishing to deny that changes occurred, the most significant of which are noted and discussed in the book, I have taken the stance of treating his work as a whole. The ultimate justification for this lies in the coherent and unitary position that we are able to draw as a result.

I am grateful to John Watling, who first taught me about Bradley while I was an undergraduate at University College, London; St Anne's College, Oxford, for giving me the opportunity to work on Bradley as a Junior Research Fellow; my colleagues at Manchester College, Oxford, for their encouragement; and to the anonymous Oxford University Press readers for their comments on the manuscript. Most of all, I would like to thank my wife, Avril, without whose patience and support this book would never have been written.

W. J. M.

Manchester College, Oxford
10 April 1993

[2] For the claim that Bradley changed his position, see Kagey (1931*a*; 1931*b*). For criticism of this view, see Segerstedt (1934), 3–15.

CONTENTS

Abbreviations   viii

1. Methodology and Metaphysics   1

2. Identity and Contradiction   28

3. Subject and Predicate   57

4. Terms and Relations   84

5. Space and Time   112

6. Idealism and the Absolute   124

7. The Absolute and its Appearances   135

8. System and Scepticism   156

   References   166

   Index   173

ABBREVIATIONS

AR   *Appearance and Reality* (1893; 2nd enlarged edn., Oxford: Clarendon Press, 1897)

CE   *Collected Essays* (Oxford: Clarendon Press, 1935)

ES   *Ethical Studies* (1876; 2nd enlarged edn., Oxford: Clarendon Press, 1927)

ETR   *Essays on Truth and Reality* (Oxford: Clarendon Press, 1914)

PL   *The Principles of Logic* (1883; 2nd enlarged edn., Oxford: Clarendon Press, 1922)

I

Methodology and Metaphysics

I T is almost inevitable that anyone schooled in contemporary Anglo-American philosophy will feel a not inconsiderable sense of dislocation should they turn to consider such a topic as the metaphysical theories of F. H. Bradley. For, notwithstanding the possibility that a deeper understanding of his thought may yield significant similarities with modern approaches, the initial impression at least is one of a great difference. His way of tackling questions seems quite alien to anything we usually encounter, his concepts obscure, and his jargon out of date; while his subject-matter, metaphysics, even if it is no longer something to dismiss out of court, is a subject that, to this day, we rarely encounter undertaken in such a bold and speculative fashion. The net result is that, although only one hundred years old, his chief metaphysical work, *Appearance and Reality*, seems more distant to those unfamiliar with it than numerous works many times its age.

It is therefore of the utmost importance, before embarking on any study of Bradleian metaphysics, to spend some time familiarizing ourselves with the nature of the project and the method of its execution, in order that we may approach it in the right spirit. Although this familiarization carries with it the danger of producing an over-sympathetic and uncritical response, unless we can see through Bradley's eyes there can be no real understanding, and thus no possibility of genuine criticism at all, sympathetic or otherwise. Moreover, a high degree of familiarity is necessary in order for us fully to recognize the differences and similarities between his thought and our own. Under the pressure of placing him in the context of their narrative, brief entries in histories of philosophy tend either to obscure or to exaggerate these comparisons. That we should familiarize ourselves with the project and approach is no mere platitude, for the task is a difficult one, and, as will become apparent, too much previous criticism has simply failed to achieve this, thus missing the mark entirely.

Before we begin this introductory investigation, some brief

remarks about the context, character, and influence of Bradley's philosophy may help to set the scene. These can then be augmented later. Bradley began his half-century-long Oxford career in 1870.[1] English philosophy was at that time predominantly empiricist, and under the influence of John Stuart Mill. But new ideas from Germany were also making themselves felt. Kant and Hegel were being rapidly assimilated, their followers, led initially by T. H. Green, forming a school that would, in a brief time, come to eclipse empiricism. Nor were they all that Germany had to offer, for those writers who had reacted against idealism, such as Herbart, Lotze, Sigwart, and Wundt, were also beginning to be read about this time.[2]

All of these influences were thrown together by Bradley into a highly original system that resists easy capture. Though at first sight idealist and Hegelian, it is also essentially realist and in the British tradition of philosophy. Though at first sight destructive, it is also highly constructive. Though at first sight metaphysical, it is also rigorously logical in its foundations. To match this singular content, Bradley developed a singular style of prose and presentation, which the poet Eliot described as, 'for his purposes . . . a perfect style'.[3] Indeed, Bradley is almost as well known today on literary grounds as on philosophical.

All this was welded together into a system that held philosophers under its spell for many years. And, even if it was later rejected as whole-heartedly as it had once been accepted, its influence lived on. The major schools of pragmatism and logical empiricism were in large part born as reactions against, and therefore cannot be fully understood except by reference to, Bradley's thought.[4] In this way he played a major role in determining the shape of contemporary philosophy.

The scene thus set, let us turn to a more detailed discussion, first

---

[1] Biographical material on Bradley, scant though it is, may be found in Taylor (1924–5; 1925; 1937); Mure (1961); Wollheim (1969), 13–15.

[2] Useful accounts of this period of philosophy in England include Passmore (1966), chs. 1–3; Manser (1983), chs. I–II. Major texts of the figures mentioned in this paragraph are Mill (1872); Kant (1929); Hegel (1977); Green (1885–8); Lotze (1884); Sigwart (1895); Herbart (1850–93), i; Wundt (1897). For a contemporary view of philosophy in Oxford, see Pattison (1876).

[3] Eliot (1975), 197. The extent of Bradley's influence on Eliot is discussed in Wollheim (1970).

[4] Passmore (1966), ch. 4; Pears (1967), ch. X; Passmore (1969); Hylton (1990).

of his methodology and secondly of the subject area that is our concern in this study, his metaphysics.

1.1 THE METHOD OF PHILOSOPHY

Bradley's approach to philosophy is unique and repays close attention. However, unlike, for instance, Bacon, Descartes, Hume, Kant, or Hegel, he never set himself up as either an expert or an innovator in philosophical methodology. Rather, his unique contribution lies in the peculiar combination that he made of a wide variety of methodological sources and the rigour with which he applied the resulting technique. It was Bradley's firm belief that, if sure reasoning leads to a conclusion, then that conclusion must be embraced, no matter how paradoxical it may seem (*PL* 685–6). Because he was not essentially a theorist of method, a full account of his approach to philosophy can be given only by examining his actual arguments in their philosophical context. None the less, he does give some brief general accounts of his procedure, which, despite their brevity, and despite the fact that philosophers are notoriously unreliable in their own self-ascriptions of method, *do* give us a reasonable place to start. In the Appendix to the second edition of *Appearance and Reality* Bradley tries to dispel some confusions that had arisen about his methodology. He says:

since I have been taken to build on assumptions which I am unable to recognize, I will here repeat what it is that I have assumed. I have assumed first that truth has to satisfy the intellect, and that what does not do this is neither true nor real. . . . And I start from the root-idea of being or experience, which is at once positive and ultimate. Then I certainly do not go on to assume about being that it must be self-contained, simple or what not?—but I proceed in another manner. I take up certain facts or truths (call them what you please) that I find are offered me, and I care very little what it is I take up. These facts or truths, as they are offered, I find my intellect rejects, and I go on to discover why it rejects them. (*AR* 509)

We find in this passage three elements of methodological importance: a criterion of truth or reality, a basic or fundamental datum for philosophizing, and a procedure for moving forwards from one idea to another. Let us take these in turn in the following sections.

1.11 *Truth and Satisfaction*

Since human beings are rational, and not merely reactive, agents, it is possible to think of the majority of their activities as purposive or directed towards some end. Aspects of life, such as the religious, the emotional, the practical, or the intellectual, may all be regarded as aiming at certain objects or states, the attainment of which constitutes their satisfaction or good, and the non-attainment of which frustrates or dissatisfies them. For instance, if the goal of religion is communion with the divine nature, then, until it finds this, the religious consciousness is frustrated and continues to strive, but, in achieving such communion, it reaches its satisfaction and is able to rest contented, be this rest either permanent or temporary.

Bradley claims that truth is what satisfies the intellect.[5] In truth, the intellect finds a rest and contentment that is its own good or end. Meaninglessness, contradiction, and falsehood, on the other hand, all produce in the intellect a sense of uneasiness or dissatisfaction, in which state it cannot remain. They leave us with a 'certain felt need' (*ETR* 311) that must be meet, and so we search for a state in which the intellect can rest contented (*AR* 509; *ETR* 1, 2, 242). Thus, in this picture of our thinking lives which Bradley paints, intellectual satisfaction plays a dual role: it is the motivating force for the dynamic movement of thought that we term 'enquiry', as well as a practical criterion of the successful completion of that enquiry—in other words, of truth.

But just what is intellectual satisfaction? Bradley says little by way of an answer to this question, but there are a number of general points which can be made about the notion. To begin with, it is satisfaction of the *intellect*. This is significant for three reasons.

First, intellectual satisfaction is to be distinguished in its mode of operation from other species of satisfaction. It is a satisfaction unique to the intellect, and not, for instance, just emotional or practical satisfaction with intellectual things.[6] The level of satisfaction in these other respects which any object is able to produce should be discounted as having no bearing on its ability to satisfy the intellect.

---

[5] For a useful discussion of intellectual satisfaction, see Candlish (1984), §II.
[6] Ibid. 244.

Secondly, because intellectual satisfaction is not the only form of satisfaction, we need to ask what kinds of objects are the most appropriate to be assessed for the level of intellectual satisfaction they yield. Intellectual satisfaction is not necessarily the highest or most important measure in all things. That this is the case may be seen, for example, by considering Bradley's discussion of morality in *Ethical Studies*.[7] He argues there that, as the call for the selfishly directed will of the individual to strive to become one with the universally directed will of society as a whole, morality is aiming at a state which undermines the very condition of its own exist-ence—namely, the separation of these two wills (*ES* 234–5). For this reason, it is held to be contradictory and thus unable to satisfy the intellect. None the less, it is able to offer, if not complete, then a significant degree of, satisfaction to the religious side of life (*ES* 314), and, with regard to the overall role that morality plays in the world, that is the more important measure. Religion is higher than philosophy in some respects, and vice versa in others. This is an important point of which we should not lose sight. If, at times during our study, philosophy seems to be the highest or the only judge, this is solely because of the kind of subjects we are in-vestigating. Bradley never loses sight of the fact that there are in life many more, and for most purposes higher, things than philosophy.

Thirdly, because intellectual satisfaction is just one form of sat-isfaction among others, it cannot achieve its final goal in isolation from those others. Bradley believed that ultimate satisfaction in any one aspect of life could not occur without the ultimate satis-faction of all aspects. Quite why he thought this will be examined later,[8] but the basic idea is that in this state, which he called the 'Absolute', the intellectual must take its place along with the other kinds of satisfaction, all submerged and transformed into the state of final and complete satisfaction. Thus, by using the idea of in-tellectual satisfaction, Bradley has a mechanism to distinguish philosophy from, and relate it to, both the other aspects of life and the higher goal of them all. In other words, it allows him to contextualize philosophy. Philosophy is but one of many limited or partial aspects of a wider reality: 'It is but one appearance among others' (*AR* 402).

[7] Useful studies of Bradley's moral philosophy include Candlish (1978); Bell (1984); Wright (1984); Johnson (1984); Nicholson (1990).
[8] See §2.11.

Part of what he intends by using the notion of *satisfaction* is to draw attention to the basic or ungrounded nature of this state. He says that, 'So far as anything satisfies, there is no possible appeal beyond it, and nothing has any rational claim against that which in itself is fully satisfied' (*ETR* 2). In the end, we accept things because they seem right to us, and that is the bottom line. So long as they seem right, we hold on to them. Of course, reasons for and against acceptance can always be given to us, but, if these make a difference, they do so only through effecting a reinforcement or change in our basic intuitions, and, moreover, they make a difference only when they are themselves accepted as correct—that is, when they seem right to us. In the end we always come down to a basic intuition, and, since there are no rules for acceptance that do not themselves have to be accepted, this gives us a picture of intellectual satisfaction as similar to some quasi-perceptual state like intellectual intuition or self-evidence.

This aspect of satisfaction is clearly demonstrated in Bradley's debate with Russell about whether anything can stand in a relation to itself (for instance, the relation of something's being the same size as itself), or, as Bradley puts it, whether there could be a relation whose terms were not diverse.[9] Russell claims to find this conceivable, while Bradley thinks it impossible. But, beyond questioning whether Russell has fully understood the suggestion and its implications, Bradley does not think the debate can go any further. 'If Mr. Russell on the other side says that he can perceive a relation where there is absolutely no diversity about the terms, I do not see how we are to argue about our difference' (*ETR* 289).

This particular disagreement between Bradley and Russell also raises the question of whether satisfaction should be thought of as an objective and shared state or as something subjective and individual. Could people really differ over what they found satisfactory, as Russell and Bradley appear to do here? Bradley is committed to thinking that, while they might seem to, in the end such disagreement is not possible, for otherwise satisfaction could not play the role of criterion for success in inter-subjective enquiry that he intends for it. Private satisfaction, however satisfactory it may seem, affords no basis for a shared science: it is 'arbitrary' (*CE* 671). Why does Bradley think this? The reason is that, as we noted

---

[9] Russell (1903), 96; *ETR* 280–8; Russell (1910), 375; *ETR* 288–92.

above, intellectual satisfaction is supposed to be separated from the influence of individual psychological factors, and the intellect is something that we all have in common, so the same things should satisfy us all. In effect, Bradley builds commonality into the definition of satisfaction, so that being shared is itself a criterion of the intellectually satisfactory. What was not shared would, for that reason, not be satisfactory. The intellectually satisfactory are, then, those things that we all cannot but accept, the indubitable.

So far intellectual satisfaction appears to play a role akin to self-evidence or intuitive correctness, but there is a further reason why Bradley favours the idiom of satisfaction. This is that, unlike self-evidence or intuitive correctness, satisfaction is a degree notion. That is crucial to Bradley, for, although he gives us a criterion of truth, he does not want to say that we ever achieve absolute truth. That is to say, he does not believe that our intellects are ever fully satisfied. Nevertheless, we experience varying degrees of satisfaction and dissatisfaction. We see how different changes produce an increase or decrease in satisfaction and we can plot the limits of these alterations, which allows us to give sense to the notions of absolute truth and falsehood, even if these are not something we ever in fact possess. Satisfaction is thus a criterion of truth, but, practically, can only ever be for us a criterion of verisimilitude.

It might be thought that we could get a more precise picture of just what intellectual satisfaction is by seeing which things in fact satisfy the intellect, and then examining what they all have in common. But here Bradley warns us off. There are, he thinks, no general criteria for what satisfies, 'as to what will satisfy I have of course no knowledge in advance' (*ETR* 311). This is a consequence of his view, discussed below,[10] that there could be no purely formal logic. Though no doubt often falling into certain general types, satisfaction is ultimately a relation between us and, not the general, but the particular or individual nature, of any item. It is thus potentially different in each case. This means that we can never give final and exhaustive rules for what will or will not satisfy the intellect. We can only look and see. We are thus prevented from giving any very precise answer to the question, what things satisfy the intellect? Candlish, for instance, suggests that what satisfies the intellect is necessary connections.[11] No doubt

---

[10] See §1.22.   [11] Candlish (1984), 244.

Bradley is satisfied with necessary connections. But, unless that just means connections we all find satisfactory, this result is far too narrow for him. He does not want to restrict the satisfactory solely to logically necessary connections, as usually defined. Thus another reason for using the idea of satisfaction here, rather than self-evidence or necessary truth, is to allow a fairly wide, and potentially infinite, range of things to fall under its scope.

Truth then satisfies the intellect, making intellectual satisfaction a criterion of truth. But what is the relation between these two notions that brings about this state of affairs? Is it a correlation of separate phenomena, or a mere identity? Taking the latter suggestion, it might be said that the link is guaranteed by definition; satisfaction is a guide to truth because truth *just is* satisfaction. Bradley's account is certainly very reminiscent of pragmatism here— for instance, of James's account of truth as whatever works or satisfies us: ' "The true", to put it very briefly, is only the expedient in the way of our thinking, just as "the right" is only the expedient in the way of our behaving.'[12] It is also reminiscent of Peirce, who in his 1877 essay 'The Fixation of Belief' says that 'The irritation of doubt causes a struggle to attain a state of belief. I shall term this struggle *Inquiry* . . . the sole object of inquiry is the settlement of opinion . . . as soon as a firm belief is reached we are entirely satisfied.'[13] It might be thought that this account is rather different from Bradley's, since, for Peirce, all we aim at is fixed belief, not truth. However, because, for Peirce, the best way of fixing belief is science, and truth is by definition what science finally yields, the two positions are closer than it might first seem.

However, Bradley's position here is not that of pragmatism. Indeed, as we shall see in the next chapter,[14] he was a fierce critic of that theory. For Bradley the link is substantial and informative, not a tautologous definition. The ability to satisfy the intellect is simply one property of truth, not its whole or defining nature, and thus only a criterion of truth. But why does he believe that truth must have the property of satisfying our intellects? Might not reality be altogether so strange or complex that a true account of it left our intellects completely unenlightened and dissatisfied? Bradley sees the force of this challenge and answers it in the following words:

---

[12] James (1907), 222.　　　[13] Peirce (1955), 10.　　　[14] See §2.14.

It is after all an enormous assumption that what satisfies us is real, and that the reality has got to satisfy us. It is an assumption tolerable, I think, only when we hold that the Universe is substantially one with each of us, and actually, as a whole, feels and wills and knows itself within us. (*ETR* 242)

Thus, for Bradley, the explanation of the link between satisfaction and truth is to be found in the ultimate identity between the subjective and the objective realms of being, or, to use a familiar metaphor, between the internal and the external worlds. This strange idea, which derives from Hegel, will be explained in greater detail in the next chapter, but the basic idea may be given here.

While there exists a difference between the subjective and the objective realms of being (a position usually described as dualism, or metaphysical realism), it seems that we must always remain sceptical about the possibility of genuine knowledge. This fact was graphically illustrated by Descartes[15] with his suggestion that there might exist a powerful and malicious demon who, by giving us the sense that we were right when we were in fact wrong, systematically led us into error about everything. So long as there exists a gap between satisfied knowing and what is known, between satisfied willing and what is willed, or between satisfied desire and what is desired, this could always be exploited in the manner of Descartes's malicious demon—that is, the sense of satisfaction could be subjective only, and nothing more than a feeling with no correspondence to reality. Only if the sense of satisfied knowledge, desire, or will is *identical* with what is known, desired, or willed can the link be guaranteed, for only then will the presence of the former logically imply and guarantee the presence of the latter.

Although it is clear how it works on paper, it is not easy to understand what this hypothesis really means. The phenomenon upon which Hegel and his followers built this theory was self-consciousness, and, although Bradley in fact rejects this (*AR* 93) as an imperfect example of the model, it none the less serves as the best illustration. In self-consciousness we know, or are aware of, our thoughts, feelings, or perceptions. But, if the latter are mental acts, self-consciousness is not some further mental act directed on them, for there is but one mental event. In the very act of thinking,

[15] Descartes (1911), Meditation I.

we know that we are thinking, and either thing is inconceivable without the other.

While Bradley's position is, as we shall see,[16] significantly different from Hegel's in a number of key respects, it is the basic Hegelian model which provides the explanation and justification of the link between truth and satisfaction. Nevertheless, it should not be seen as epistemologically prior to, or establishing, that link. No theory about the criterion of truth could ever be accepted as true unless we were already in possession of some criterion of truth. Instead, thinks Bradley, we must simply *assume* the link between truth and satisfaction, and, on the basis of that assumption, find a theory that explains and justifies it. Thus, with perfect consistency, Bradley claims that we assume that it is true that satisfaction is a guide to truth because we are compelled to—that is to say, because we find this thesis itself to be satisfactory. Thus Bradley says, to complete the passage partially quoted above, 'I have assumed first that truth has to satisfy the intellect, and that what does not do this is neither true nor real. This assumption I can defend only by showing that any would-be objector assumes it also.' (*AR* 509).

1.12   *Immediate Experience*

Let us consider the next element of Bradley's method—that is, the 'root-idea' of being or experience, spoken of above. To say that we should start with 'being' is singularly unhelpful unless we already have a theory of what really exists. Of far greater interest, on the other hand, is the claim that we should take, as the basic datum of philosophy, 'experience', or, as Bradley expresses it alternatively, 'feeling'.

In view of the fact that Bradley is so often represented as a rationalist, in direct opposition to the native British tradition of empiricism, it may be felt surprising to find this here. None the less Bradley is quite adamant about the importance of feeling. It is our only starting-point and our only connection with reality. For instance, he says that 'The real is that which is known in presentation or intuitive knowledge. It is what we encounter in feeling or perception' (*PL* 44), and 'Nothing in the end is real but

---

[16] See §2.11.

what is felt' (*ETR* 190). Again he claims that 'Apart from the immediacy of "this" and "now" we never have, or can have, reality. The real, to be real, must be felt' (*ETR* 190 n.). Thus, for Bradley, experience was a crucial touchstone with reality. This fact about his philosophy has rarely been recognized,[17] and thus to do so necessitates a re-evaluation of his position in the history of philosophy.

However, it should be pointed out that at no stage does Bradley mean here to appeal to what might be described as common-sense experience, the kind of window on to reality that we pre-reflectively suppose ourselves to enjoy. He recognizes too well the undeniable truth that our everyday perceptual experience of the world is not simply a product of what the senses give us, but is mediated or tainted by our own input and conceptualization. Ordinary experience is not just passively given to us but also actively constructed by us. Primordial feeling is a wholly preconceptual state and, since common-sense experience is utterly ridden with conceptualization, quite unlike anything we ordinarily experience. To put it another way, if common-sense experience is a stage on our journey from immediate experience to the Absolute, we have already travelled no less far from our starting-point than we still have to travel in order to reach our goal.

The base data to which Bradley thinks we must appeal differs from everyday sense experience in two ways. First, it is wider in scope than, for example, just the data of our five senses. It includes sensations, feelings, emotions, will, desire, and thoughts— in short, 'everything of which in any sense I am aware' (*ETR* 189). It is, we might say, the whole life of experience. Secondly, it also differs in *nature* from everyday experience. It is, he thinks, an immediate whole of feeling with difference but no distinction. It 'contains diversity' but 'is not parted by relations' (*AR* 141); 'It is all one blur with differences, that work and that are felt, but are not discriminated' (*CE* 216). It is prior to all division, even that between self and not-self, being 'a state as yet without either an object or subject' (*ETR* 194). It is also prior to that distinction between concept or knowledge and object or existence, it is 'a knowing and being in one' (*ETR* 159). Other subsequent

---

[17] The importance of experience is recognized in Mack (1945); Cresswell (1977; 1979); Bradley (1984); McHenry (1992). Cresswell, however, goes to the opposite extreme of over-emphasizing its significance.

philosophers, such as James, Bergson, and Whitehead, have all put
forward similar views, but the earlier model and source is Hegel's
psychology, as developed in the *Phenomenology of Spirit*,[18] and
Bradley explicitly acknowledges this debt (*ETR* 153, *AR* 508 n.).

While feeling is our only point of contact with reality, it is not
itself either real or consistent (*AR* 407). Feeling is subject to internal incoherences, which cause it to break up and change—or,
as Bradley puts it, to transcend itself—into thought. What was felt
becomes thought or conceptualized. Once it has been conceptualized, the initial incoherence can be recognized. In thinking, we
break it up into what Bradley calls its content and its existence,
what it is and that it is. But this allows us to see that its content
was not really in accord with its existence, that it was not quite
the harmonious union of knowing and being that it first seemed
to be. The problem is that it is finite and limited, but this aspect
of its nature can be understood only in contrast with, and hence
by reference to, the wider reality of which it is but a portion. In
this sense, thinks Bradley, its content, or what it is, transcends the
limited boundaries of its existence. To specify it fully, we need to
appeal to more than it really is. This tension causes us to separate
content from existence, and, in searching for a wider reality to
match our expanded content, to enter the world of thought or
judgement. Feeling is thus logically prior to thought. Bradley also
thinks that it might well characterize a temporally earlier stage of
our individual or social development (*ETR* 174, cf. *CE* XII), but
does not press the point.

More certain is that, in the very act of beginning to think,
immediate experience is thereby transcended. Thus immediate
experience is not something we, as thinking beings, ever ordinarily
encounter. We may seem to grasp it in aesthetic experience, but in
the end Bradley doubts this (*AR* 410–12). Nevertheless, although
we transcend it, it is not wholly lost or left behind. It remains
throughout as the foundation of all our subsequent thinking (*ETR*
160); that is to say, Bradley believes that the forms of ordinary
experience can only be understood as having evolved from this.
An analogy may help here. Although a musical theme may never
be heard, it is present as the foundation of the variations we
do hear. Similarly, although we may never express the phonetic

---

[18] James (1910); Bergson (1911); Whitehead (1929); Hegel (1977).

elements or the rules of language, they are the present foundation of any language that we do speak.

I suggested that it was mistaken to contrast Bradley's position with that of empiricism, but this claim might be objected to. If we understand empiricism as the thesis that all knowledge comes from experience, then, in positing this bizarre state of feeling, Bradley seems to be contravening the basic tenet of empiricism. It goes well beyond anything we ever ordinarily experience, and, as such, how do we know that it even exists?

Yet this objection is misguided, and rests on a confusion that has dogged the history of empiricism. We might think of empiricism as containing both a methodological and an epistemological component. The methodological component (1) says, All inquiry starts from experience. The epistemological component (2) says, All knowledge is grounded in or justified by experience. The confusion is to suppose that the word 'experience' means the same in both cases. There is no reason why it must, and it is implausible to suppose that it does. In the first it clearly means ordinary experience, for, unless we are born with innate ideas or knowledge, there is no other place from which to start. But why should we suppose it means the same in the second case? Why should the data we happen to possess be those from which reality is in fact built up? Might they not contain impurities put in by us? If so, then, although we start with ordinary experience, we have to remove our additions. This is a matter of analysis and argument. Not even traditional empiricism believes that the foundational data is the data of ordinary experience. Simple ideas, or sense data, which they take to be the ground of knowledge, are not what is given in ordinary experience. What Bradley is doing here is essentially no different. He starts with ordinary experience, but the data of ordinary experience must be analysed in thought to find the real experiential data from which our knowledge of reality is built. Of course, he differs from traditional empiricism in his belief about the extent to which ordinary experience has been contaminated and thus in the amount of work that needs to be done to get to the basic data, but this is only a difference of degree. Thus we see that only on a very peculiar definition of empiricism that identifies the ground of knowledge with everyday experience would Bradley fail to be an empiricist; but such a definition would exclude most, if not all, of those traditionally classed as empiricists.

There is even a sense in which we could say that Bradley is *more* of an empiricist than the traditional British empiricists, for it could be argued that they have not gone far enough back in their search for the basic data. To find the ultimate foundation of knowledge, we need to look for an input that has all conceptualization removed. It is for this reason that Cresswell,[19] quite correctly, characterizes Bradley as a hyper-empiricist. He searches out the purest data of experience and bases everything on this.

Feeling is important to Bradley, not only as the origin or ground of philosophy, but also as its terminus or goal. As we have already seen, any final satisfaction of thought must also be a satisfaction of feeling (will, sense, desire, etc.) as well as thought. The Absolute is therefore a state of feeling or experience, making immediate experience into a kind of anticipation of the life of the Absolute (*AR* 141). But, although something of the same fundamental kind as the Absolute, it is a flawed anticipation, for unlike the Absolute it is, as we saw above, finite and limited, and thus subject to contradictions.

It is, however, an accurate picture of the Absolute in so far as it is not simply a system of concepts or thoughts. This is the crucial difference between Bradley and Hegel that we hinted at above. Like Hegel, Bradley thinks that thought and reality are not separate things, but, unlike Hegel, he thinks that reality is more than just thought. That the real is simply the rational strikes him as a cold and lifeless idea (*PL* 591). This was the basic Hegelian principle he could not accept, and why he was therefore reluctant to call himself a Hegelian (*PL*, p. x). He agrees that the real is the rational, but thinks it is also much more—it is feeling as well. This break from pure Hegelianism and move towards realism are crucial elements of Bradley's philosophy, the full significance of which has not been appreciated in many of the standard accounts of his thought.[20]

1.13   *Ideal Experiment*

Finally let us examine the third element of Bradley's method, his strategy for proceeding from one idea to another in philosophy.

---

[19] Cresswell (1977), 170.   [20] See ch. 6.

He is quite clear about the method he follows, and explains it in the following way:

I will . . . begin by noticing some misunderstandings as to the method employed in ultimate inquiry by writers like myself. There is an idea that we start, consciously or unconsciously, with certain axioms, and from these reason downwards. This idea to my mind is baseless. The method actually followed may be called in the main the procedure used by Hegel, that of a direct ideal experiment made on reality. What is assumed is that I have to satisfy my theoretical want, or, in other words, that I resolve to think. And it is assumed that, if my thought is satisfied with itself, I have, with this, truth and reality. But as to what will satisfy I have of course no knowledge in advance. My object is to get before me what will content a certain felt need, but the way and the means are to be discovered only by trial and rejection. The method clearly is experimental. (*ETR* 311)

There are a number of points that may usefully be drawn out for comment from this passage.

To begin with, Bradley tells us how he does *not* proceed. On numerous occasions (*PL* 530; *ETR* 289, 316 n.) he insists that his method is not axiomatic—that is to say, that he does not start from a limited number of general truths and deduce from them a larger body of more detailed principles. What he is objecting to here is the approach of epistemological foundationalism. According to this way of doing philosophy, given perhaps its clearest exposition in the philosophy of Descartes,[21] we must begin from indubitable foundations upon which we gradually build up our structure. This is rejected because for Bradley there are no truths with the character necessary to act as epistemological foundations. No claim is in itself indubitably true, but acquires this character only by its place within the whole system. The structure of Bradley's thought thus forms an interconnected web or circle, in which all propositions mutually support each other, the burden of justification being shared out equally among them. He begins *The Principles of Logic* by claiming that there is no one accepted order (*PL* 1). We can start where we like, working our way out until we have covered the whole system. Where we choose to start is a pragmatic affair, for justification lies, not in where we start from, but in the way, as we progress outwards, we take in more and

[21] Descartes (1911).

more of reality. On this point, Bradley would have agreed with the philosopher Bosanquet, who put this idea very well when he claimed that knowledge is 'a system of such a character that A and B prove each other when put together, though neither is certain when isolated'.[22] Exactly why Bradley thought that this was the case we shall try to show in the course of this study, but for the moment it will suffice to note the idea's attractiveness.

One consequence of this non-axiomatic method is that it makes exposition of his philosophy difficult. There is no obvious place to start, without taking in the whole. An example of this is the case of immediate experience discussed above. We presented it as the ground or starting-point of his philosophy, but, while this is true, it is also something arrived at through argument and reflection, and hence grounded in and supported by that very same philosophy. Another example, that we shall meet at the end of this chapter, is the relation between logic and metaphysics. In view of this fact it might seem that a better way to approach his philosophy would be as a whole system, beginning with the widest view and then exploring the detail. This would be the case were Bradley really true to his word. But in fact, although all are interconnected, some of his claims *are* more foundational than others. So his thought *does* have a basic structure. We shall explore this in Chapters 2–4. None the less, it remains true that, in giving any account of his philosophy, it is often the case that things do not become fully clear until later, when a different but interlocking piece of the jigsaw is added.

Having told us how he does not work, he goes on to tell us how he does proceed. He claims that the connections between elements of his thought are 'experimental', or that he advances by 'ideal experiment'. What does this mean?[23] And how, if at all, does it differ from the notions we would more normally expect to find here? Bradley gives no general account of what ideal experiment is, but we can learn something about it by examining some examples.

The term occurs most prominently in his discussion of inference.[24] He claims that 'Inference is an experiment, an ideal experiment which gains fresh truth' (*PL* 492). His general view of

---

[22] Bosanquet (1885*a*), 265.
[23] For a useful discussion of ideal experiment, see Candlish (1984), §III.
[24] For a useful discussion of Bradley's theory of inference, see Allard (1989).

inference is that it has three elements: starting phenomena or premises, some intellectual manipulation of that material, producing a result attributed to it (*PL* 256). All inference then involves some kind of mental operation. 'This operation is an ideal experiment upon something which is given, and the result of this process is invariably ascribed to the original *datum*' (*PL* 431). He gives us examples of different types of operation or experiment, but one of the curiosities of Bradley's theory of inference is that he refuses to supply any 'fixed models for reasoning', or full lists of types of inference (*PL* 268). This is partly because he sees inference as a skill, so that what it can do depends on who is doing it (*PL* 259), but also because he refuses to set out beforehand any limits on what activities could take the middle place of this triad (*PL* 267). Although in the most general sense all operations either analytically divide or synthetically combine ideas (*PL* 450), there is no limit to the number of different possible operations or experiments. There are an infinite number of possible connections or special relations (*PL* 268). This is why he gives us no general account of what they are, which shows that they cannot be simply logical truths or deductive patterns. That would be too limiting.

They cannot even be limited to the sphere of inference. Inference is ideal experiment, but ideal experiment is not simply inference. Supposal, or hypothetical statement, is also an ideal experiment (*PL* 86). In supposal we try out an idea on reality to see what the consequence is. Negation involves ideal experiment as well (*PL* 120–1). In a negative judgement on thing repels or excludes another, but this activity occurs only in the mental realm between ideas.

Nevertheless, considering the examples that he does give allows us to make at least some general comments about ideal experiments. They are *ideal* in the sense that they concern meanings or ideas. 'This process is on the one hand *ideal*, in the sense that it advances on the strength of a connection between universals' (*PL* 441).

By calling them experiments Bradley wants to imply several things. First, he wants to stress that, although ideal, they are questions put to reality or the world. In this sense the experimental outcomes are correct or incorrect, they are not just a matter of our intuitions. This is what lies behind his alternative definition of inference as the 'ideal self-development of an object' (*PL* 597).

Another reason for calling them experiments is that we cannot guarantee their results. He says, 'It is clear, I think, that when trying experiments in the actual world by combining and dividing real things, or by drawing upon paper, we may be surprised by qualities which we did not anticipate. And the same must be true of ideal experiment' (*PL* 397). This is because they are about reality, not merely the consequences of a pre-formed deductive structure.

A third point in calling them experiments is to contrast them with reasoning or inference. Of course, since some experiments *are* inferences, the intended contrast here is not with inference *per se*, but rather with the common understanding that sees inference as a process involving the deduction of a chain of specific consequences from assumed general axioms. There are two differences to note here. First, Bradley wants to stress that his operations are individual and self-supporting particulars, not instances or examples of generalized and validating principles or relations (*PL* 530). This is why there can be no exhaustive rules for them; the attempt to characterize them exhaustively would be the attempt to characterize a 'completed infinity' (*PL* 268). Secondly, he also wants to imply that in making his steps he is operating as far as possible without presuppositions. If you set the conditions of inference axiomatically, then you determine all possible outcomes. But, if you simply take up phenomena and try to see what happens when you operate on them, even if you are careful in what you select, the level of presupposition is lower. For instance, regarding the question of relations with identical terms that we considered above,[25] the idea is that we simply take an ordinary common-sense relation, without assuming anything else, and just try to see what happens if we remove its diversity.

Since ideal experiments have no formal patterns or exhaustive set of rules, but none the less claim to be true of reality, a question naturally arises concerning their validity. In the end, all Bradley can say is that they are self-evident or ultimately satisfactory, and he must assume that what is ultimately satisfactory is true. This is not unreasonable. It is the attitude that we must all take over the axioms of our system. Bradley is simply extending it to the whole corpus of reasoning itself. Indeed, in view of the fact that most systems can be axiomatized in numerous different ways, the

[25] See p. 6.

extension is attractive, for in such cases it is hard to see what privileged status the chosen axioms can really possess.[26] This assumption of validity is given explanatory (although, as we have seen, not evidential) support through Bradley's theory of the identity of the subjective and the objective realms (*ETR* 242) that we discussed above, and his corresponding belief that inference concerns the things themselves as much as it does our thoughts about them.

Bringing all this together, we see then that an ideal experiment is a thought experiment performed on reality and guaranteed by self-evidence. It is thus wider than mere deduction.

There are two further points in the passage we quoted above that need to be brought out. The first is Bradley's claim to be pursuing a method which is essentially that of Hegel. We need to ask, what relation, if any, does this bear to the Hegelian method? It is the emphasis on particular concrete inferences which are as much movements of reality as movements of thought that here makes him identify his procedure with Hegel's. For Hegel, too, inferences were developments of reality itself, and consequently not formal, but containing a particular concrete content. For both philosophers the way to do philosophy is not to go at things with some instrument or tool, but to stand back and let reality unfold itself. Hegel, of course, believed that this is something which occurs dialectically, and Bradley[27] could accept this only with considerable reservations.

The second point is his description of his own method as 'trial and rejection'. In part this is just another way of saying that it is experimental, and that the results must be settled by an unpredictable reality, not by us. The claim may, however, be combined with others (*PL*, pp. ix–x; *AR*, pp. vii–viii) to give us a view of his entire philosophy as one of criticism or scepticism. Of all his methodological self-ascriptions, this is the most puzzling. While *Appearance and Reality* contains much that is destructive or critical, it appears also to contain as much or more that is bold and constructive. This is a fundamental paradox of his philosophy, but, rather than discuss it here, let us first look at his system and then assess the case. We shall therefore devote the last chapter of

---

[26] Cf. Wittgenstein's view of inference (Wittgenstein (1961), 5.11–5.143), and Schopenhauer's view of geometry (Schopenhauer (1969), i. 171–4).

[27] See pp. 54–5.

our study to this question. This brings us to the end of our discussion of his methodology.

1.2 THE NATURE OF METAPHYSICS

Leaving this somewhat brief account of Bradley's methodology, let us turn to consider his view of metaphysics—the subject-matter of this study. Bradley begins *Appearance and Reality* with an attempt to define metaphysics:

> We may agree, perhaps, to understand by metaphysics an attempt to know reality as against mere appearance, or the study of first principles or ultimate truths, or again the effort to comprehend the universe, not simply piecemeal or by fragments, but somehow as a whole. (*AR* 1)

It would be desirable at this stage to give a full explication of these three definitions, demonstrating how they describe but different aspects of the same exercise. Unfortunately this is hardly possible, for the form that these definitions take is largely a consequence of the metaphysical system they define. Thus they become fully accessible to our understanding only at the end of that system. Nevertheless, it is possible to give a brief sketch of what Bradley means by metaphysics. This will be filled in as we continue with the study.

1.21 *The Metaphysical Quest*

In describing metaphysics as the pursuit of ultimate truth or first principles, Bradley wishes to bring out its relation to all other knowledge. It is simultaneously the terminus of all thought, that beyond which we cannot go in thought, and the ground or foundation of all our thinking. It is the final and highest knowledge we can arrive at, but at the same time the base which sets the initial and boundary conditions of all knowledge. This is not the contradiction that it might first seem, since we, as human beings, are compelled to start in the middle of knowledge, taking up what appear to be facts about the world as it seems to us, and gradually work out from there to the edge. But what is the criterion for describing facts as lying on the edge of, or setting the parameters for, reality? One common criterion is what might be called 'depth'.

In this sense we might ask, what are the ultimate constituents or foundational building blocks of reality? This would give us one way of understanding the second definition of metaphysics, for, in seeking depth, we are contrasting the surface appearance with the deep reality. However, for Bradley the important criterion is not so much depth as what might be called 'breadth'. According to this way of viewing things, metaphysical truth is to be contrasted not so much with superficial or surface truth, as with partial or limited truth. There are many statements which hold good for the most part, but under some conditions and in some respects break down. They fail to take into account all conditions and contexts. Ultimate truth takes everything into account. It leaves nothing out that could affect its truth. It is the culmination of thought. This explains Bradley's third definition of metaphysics as an understanding of the whole rather than its parts. Nor does it leave behind the second, for Bradley does not *oppose* breadth to depth; rather he thinks that insufficient depth is just one kind of narrow and limited view. Thus we extend the notion of appearance to any limited view of things. All this will be made clearer as we progress.

But is metaphysics thus conceived really possible? Bradley thinks that it is possible, because it is inevitable. Every world-view carries with it its own metaphysics, the only question being whether this is explicitly recognized or not. Even someone who says metaphysics cannot be done 'is a brother metaphysician with a rival theory of first principles' (*AR* 1). Bradley is appealing here to an argument, often raised against Kant, and common since his time,[28] that any attempt to state a limit to knowledge is already to pass beyond that limit, for how can we specify what cannot be thought without thinking it? It is curious in view of what he says elsewhere about the limits of knowledge to find Bradley endorsing this argument. The key to this puzzle is given in chapter XV of *Appearance and Reality*. Thought does not assert the existence of something beyond itself; rather it points to such a state, for to assert it would indeed be to pass beyond thought itself.[29]

But even if metaphysics is possible, why should we study it? Part of its justification is as an antidote to dogmatism. Commonly accepted philosophical views have a tendency to collapse under close metaphysical inspection. 'That is one reason why I think that

---

[28] See e.g. Wittgenstein (1961), 3.   [29] See §2.11.

metaphysics, even if it end in total scepticism, should be studied by a certain number of persons' (*AR* 5). Bradley sees scepticism as a prime component of metaphysics and a large part of his task. He saw his work as largely critical or destructive, as clearing the ground for a system he felt unable to provide.

Yet that is not the real reason why we study metaphysics. Since the measure of truth is intellectual satisfaction, ultimate truth yields ultimate intellectual satisfaction, and, not surprisingly, since it gives us ultimate satisfaction, metaphysics answers a basic need in us. This in itself is sufficient justification for pursuing it. Metaphysics is just one of the out-workings of this basic need, and all are justified as fundamental demands of the kind of creatures we are.

When poetry, art, and religion have ceased wholly to interest, or when they show no longer any tendency to struggle with ultimate problems and to come to an understanding with them; when the sense of mystery and enchantment no longer draws the mind to wander aimlessly and to love it knows not what; when, in short, twilight has no charm—then metaphysics will be worthless. (*AR* 3)

Just how the metaphysical quest can answer a basic desire in us is explained in more detail in the following passage.

All of us, I presume, more or less, are led beyond the region of ordinary facts. Some in one way and some in others, we seem to touch and have communion with what is beyond the visible world. In various manners we find something higher, which both supports and humbles, both chastens and transports us. And, with certain persons, the intellectual effort to understand the universe is a principal way of thus experiencing the Deity. No one, probably, who has not felt this, however differently he might describe it, has ever cared much for metaphysics. And, wherever it has been felt strongly, it has been its own justification. (*AR* 5)

But, at times, Bradley suggests that it is not just the drive to study metaphysics, but also our metaphysical results themselves, that are influenced in this way. He notoriously quotes in the introduction to *Appearance and Reality* from his book of Aphorisms, 'Metaphysics is the finding of bad reasons for what we believe upon instinct, but to find these reasons is no less an instinct' (*AR*, p. x). Later he says of one of his doctrines, 'If I were not convinced of its truth on the ground of metaphysics, I should still believe it upon instinct. And, though I am willing to concede that my metaphysics may be wrong, there is, I think, nothing which could persuade me that my instinct is not right' (*ETR* 268).

Some critics have taken such statements to suggest that perhaps Bradley's fundamental positions are ones of faith or ungrounded presumption, lacking any compelling theoretical support.[30] Such conclusions seem, however, to be over-hasty. Bradley is not claiming that his principles are just assumed or that he offers no arguments for them. He is simply pointing out in a typically honest fashion a fact that everyone ought to acknowledge, that in the end we cannot but go where we feel led, or accept what seems right to us. At the end of the day we are all guided by our intuitions, and it is not only dishonest, but foolish, to deny this, for there is no other way of proceeding. He makes this point about his methodology quite clear in a letter to Russell:

I think I understand what you say as to the way in which you philosophise. I imagine that it is the right way and that its promises are never illusions, though they may not be kept to the letter. There is something perhaps in the whole of things that one feels is wanting when one considers the doctrines before one, and (as happens elsewhere) one feels that one knows what one wants and that what one wants is there—if only one could find it. And for my part I believe that one does find it more or less. And yet still I must believe that one never does or can find the whole in all its aspects, and that there never after all will be a philosopher who did not reach his truth, after all, except by some partiality and one-sidedness— and that, far from mattering, this is the right and the only way.[31]

1.22   *Metaphysics and Logic*

Further light may be shed upon Bradley's conception of metaphysics by placing it in its wider context, and examining what he considers to be its relations to the many other activities of human life. Metaphysics is the pursuit of ultimate intellectual satisfaction, but we have already seen that, for Bradley, there are kinds of pursuit with species of satisfaction, other than just the intellectual. For instance, there are the pursuits of religion, art, politics, and morals, as well as the practical sides of life. Intellectual aims are not necessarily the fundamental or the highest kind, and in the ultimate reality they must take their place beside the other non-intellectual

---

[30] Saxena (1967), 15–18; Candlish (1984), 263.
[31] Russell (1975), 235–6.

sides of our life. He says that, if philosophy is higher in some respects, in others it is lower (*AR* 402).

Moreover, metaphysics is not the only intellectual pursuit. Therefore, we need to ask what is the relation between metaphysics and the other pursuits of the intellect? In most cases Bradley's answer to this question is simple: the relation is that of a higher to a lesser truth. Next to metaphysics, other pursuits of the intellect offer merely partial or limited truth, though they are none the less valuable in their own sphere for that. The sciences, for instance, although they cannot contribute to the advancement of absolute truth, play an important role in predicting and explaining the occurrence of actual phenomena, something metaphysics cannot do.[32]

However, there is one particular subject which bears an especially close relation to metaphysics, and can tell us much about it. That subject is logic, an area in which Bradley did a great deal of pioneering work. What is the relation between this and his metaphysics? Although the relationship between logic and metaphysics is an extremely important one, Bradley never makes it very clear.[33] He does not, for instance, clearly distinguish between them or explain fully how they bear on each other. But this is no oversight on his part; rather, we are forcing a certain model on him. He does not distinguish between or relate them, because, in the end, he does not believe that there is any ultimate difference between them. With regard to the interface between logic and metaphysics, 'I confess', he says, 'I am not sure where Logic begins or ends' (*PL*, p. ix). In the *Principles of Logic* he tries as far as possible to avoid metaphysics, but admits that in the end this is not something that can ever really be achieved (*PL* 552). No distinction between them is an ultimately tenable one. Bosanquet, the logician with whom he has most in common, puts the point far more clearly, but in a way that Bradley would certainly accept, saying,

I entertain no doubt that in content Logic is one with metaphysics, and differs if at all simply in mode of treatment—in tracing the evolution of knowledge in the light of its value and import, instead of attempting to summarize its value and import apart from the details of its evolution.[34]

---

[32] Dawes Hicks (1925); Delany (1971); Mander (1991).
[33] For a good discussion of the relation between logic and metaphysics, see Bedell (1971).   [34] Bosanquet (1911), i. 232.

To us the idea that logic and metaphysics are a single subject is a quite strange one. Bradley finds this to be the case because he holds a very different view of logic from that which we favour today. Like Hegel, he does not think that logic can be purely formal. Since its ideas and judgements are all true of reality, and its inferences concrete developments of that reality, logic must not be seen as a system of merely abstract ideas in purely formal relations. The reason why he holds this view of logic is that ultimately, like Hegel, he thinks that thought and reality are identical. Logic describes the nature and laws of thought, metaphysics describes the nature and laws of reality, but, if these two things are really the same, any difference between the subjects is just one of emphasis or perspective, not content.

As we have already noted, the statement that Bradley accepted the Hegelian identity of thought and reality has to be qualified, for he is not an orthodox Hegelian. Hegel famously expressed his theory in the dictum that what is reasonable is actual and that what is actual is reasonable.[35] Bradley cannot quite accept this. He does not believe there is anything in thought which is not also in reality, but he is clear that reality contains more than thought. Yet this difference does not seriously affect his Hegelian view of the relation between logic and metaphysics sketched above, for, while Bradley is adamant that reality is more than just rational thought, he also believes, curiously enough, that there is no need to go outside of thought in order to find it. Thought is at least a part of reality, and it is a consequence of Bradley's theory of relations (to be discussed in Chapter 4) that the whole is, in some sense, present in each of its parts, be they thought, volition, feeling, or whatever. He puts it this way: 'in thinking we find all reality. But in the same way the whole reality can as well be found in feeling or in volition. Each is one element in the whole, or the whole in one of its aspects' (*AR* 154; cf. *PL* 600). In this way, although thought is narrower than reality, their respective studies (that is, logic and metaphysics) may still be said to deal with the same subject-matter.

This means that any distinction between logic and metaphysics can only be a practical one. We already mentioned that, in the *Principles of Logic*, he tried, as far as possible, 'to avoid metaphysics'

---

[35] Hegel (1975), 9.

(*PL* 591 n.), but this is a merely pragmatic stance. He recognizes that when he suggests that the book could be criticized for having both too much and too little metaphysics (*PL*, pp. x–xi). It all depends on how you look at it and your purposes in making the distinction. In the end this is a distinction not of subject-matter but of depth: to describe how we think is logic, but the deeper we go the more we are really doing metaphysics. Or, to put it another way, we might say that logic describes the conditions necessary for adequate thought, but considerations of their fulfilment are a matter for metaphysics.[36]

In view of the kind of distinction to be made between them, we not unnaturally find that the relations between metaphysics and logic run both ways. Bradley's metaphysics dictates his logical principles, but it also acts as ultimate ground of, and justification for, them. Although these cannot be fully understood until we have gone deeper into his system, some examples may help to give the general picture of this reciprocal relationship. For instance, his denial of metaphysical plurality implies the logical form of judgements as true, not of different subjects, but of reality in general (*PL* 630). Also we see that the validity of inference is a question that ultimately can be justified only by a metaphysical position (*PL* 579–91).

But his logical investigations also imply, ground, and justify his metaphysical theories. For instance, his position on negation and contradiction entails the denial of plurality (*AR* 509), and his view of ideas or meaning entails his holism (*PL* 11). Thus we have to approach his metaphysics through his logic. Indeed it has been suggested that his metaphysics is a closed book to anyone unfamiliar with his logic.[37]

Although the relation between logic and metaphysics goes both ways, because of his un-Hegelian stance indicated above, it is not simply symmetrical. Since the fundamental nature of reality determines the nature of thought, his logic flows from his metaphysics. But, because thought is not straightforwardly identical with reality, we cannot simply read off his metaphysics from his logic. Logic does make demands on reality, but, because it itself is something less than reality, it needs to be seen as functioning rather like an arrow in this respect. It points to its demands, but cannot

---

[36] Allard (1986), 30–1.   [37] Mackenzie (1894), 306.

explain in detail how they are met, for they are met only in a world beyond thought.

To say that logic grounds metaphysics and metaphysics grounds logic may look circular, but that need not worry anyone except a foundationalist. Really this intimate relation between logic and metaphysics provides another illustration of the non-foundational nature of Bradley's thought that we discussed above. The burden of support is not held by one side only, but shared mutually. The significance of this mutual implication for us in this study is that there can be no understanding of Bradley's metaphysics without a grasp of its logical foundations. This will be our task in the next chapter.

2

Identity and Contradiction

IN this chapter we shall examine the logical foundations of Bradley's philosophy, although, as we saw at the end of the previous chapter, in the last resort these may not be regarded as fundamentally any different from its metaphysical foundations. In particular we shall look at two topics: Bradley's account of the relation between thought and reality, and his core beliefs about the basic logical structure of reality. Both of these matters are of central importance to the discussion in the rest of the book.

2.1 THOUGHT AND REALITY

Thoughts which purport to describe things may stand to reality either in the relation of truth or in the relation of falsehood. But what is truth? What is the relationship between a true thought and the reality it is true of? If anything is foundational to Bradley's philosophy, it is this question. The theory he gives stands central to, and has consequences that radiate outwards through, his thought. We shall consider first his own theory about the nature of truth, and then, since there has been much misinterpretation over what his position was, some of the other accounts that are commonly attributed to him, and how he in fact stands to them.

At this stage a word is in order about the precise way in which Bradley frames the question of truth. All of his discussions replace the general talk of 'thought' as the bearer of truth with the more specific term 'judgement'. It is tempting to suppose that 'judgement' for Bradley plays the role of 'proposition' in modern philosophy. In so far as the intended contrast is with 'sentence', this is correct: different sentences, for instance in different languages, could be used to make the same judgement, just as they might express the same proposition. However, like Hegel, Bradley does not believe that 'proposition' and 'judgement' may be taken as simply equivalent. The former, in so far as it is considered in detachment from its possible employment, is thought by Bradley to be too abstract for use as the fundamental vehicle of meaning in logic.[1]

2.11 The Identity Theory of Truth

Bradley's theory of truth is extremely unusual, and rather perplexing. But, notwithstanding these facts, there is no excuse for misinterpreting him, for there can be no doubt as to what he actually says.[2] Although it is repeated in numerous other places, the theory is most clearly expressed in his *Essays on Truth and Reality*, where he says:

> The division of reality from knowledge and of knowledge from truth must in any form be abandoned. And the only way of exit from the maze is to accept the remaining alternative. Our one hope lies in taking courage to embrace the result that reality is not outside truth. The identity of truth knowledge and reality, whatever difficulty that may bring, must be taken as necessary and fundamental. (*ETR* 112–13)

In order to understand his meaning in this passage we need to note that there is an ambiguity in the word 'truth'. The word can refer either to a true proposition or set of such propositions (as in 'Are you telling me the truth?'), or to the particular property held by such a proposition or propositions (as in 'The opposite of falsity is truth'). When Bradley speaks of the identity of truth and reality he has in mind the former sense: a proposition or set of propositions, if true, is identical with the reality it is, or they are, true of. Thus we might say that truth, in the second sense, consists in the identity of the truth-bearer with its reality.

It is his adherence to this theory of truth that explains why he often speaks somewhat indifferently of 'truth or reality' (*AR*, chs XV, XXIV), and claims that 'It is impossible . . . to deal with truth apart from an examination of the nature of reality' (*ETR* 310). In the end these two things are for him identical, or at least coincident.

But why does he think that this is the case? It is, after all, a very strange theory. There is no chance of our understanding this theory without our understanding the prototype from which it derives.

---

[1] *PL* 640. See below, pp. 62–3, 143–4; cf. Manser (1983), 36, 206.
[2] Correct accounts of his theory of truth may be found in Segerstedt (1934), 29–32; Candlish (1989); Baldwin (1991).

That is the basic model of Hegel's philosophy—namely, the identity between subject and object, or, as it is alternatively expressed, between knower and known—which, subject to some very important qualifications discussed below, Bradley took over as his own. We have already had occasion to mention this theory, and two of the common arguments for it.[3]

The first argument is from the possibility of scepticism. So long as thought and reality remain separated, Hegel thinks that nothing could ever bridge the gap between them, making human knowledge impossible. Bradley echoes this argument: unless what we know is nothing but our knowing, the pursuit of philosophy is hopeless:

Apart from the belief that the ultimate and absolute Real is actually present and working within us, what are we to think of the claim that reality is in the end that which satisfies one or more of us? It seems a lunatic dream. . . . The ideas and wishes of 'fellows such as I crawling between heaven and earth', how much do they count in the march or the drift of the Universe? (*ETR* 243)

But the theory is more than just epistemically expedient, it was felt by many neo-Hegelians to be unavoidable, and this is where the second argument comes in. How could there be any reality other than thought? It was commonly argued at this time that the notion of such a reality beyond thought was contradictory, for to postulate it would be to think it. Even to place limits on thought is already to pass beyond those limits. Bradley himself accepts this argument, and, as we have already seen, uses it to attack those who deny the possibility of metaphysics (*AR* 1, 114).

In calling Hegel's system a model for the identity theory of truth, I do not mean to suggest that Hegel himself held this theory of truth.[4] For on Hegel's system *all* thought, and not just true thought, is held to be identical with reality. In order for it to function as a basis for the identity theory of truth, the system must be modified so that this is something which holds of thoughts only in so far as they are true. But Hegel's system does function as a model in the sense that it tells us why it might be supposed, and what might be meant by saying, that true thoughts are identical

[3] See pp. 8–9, 21–2.
[4] Hegel's theory of truth is expressed in Hegel (1975), §§24, 172, 213.

with reality. Bradley's modifications to Hegel's system are best understood by looking at his worries about it.

There can be no doubt that Hegel's theory is a counter-intuitive one. To our way of thinking, thought and reality are so different that talk of their identity seems nonsense. How could an idea in my mind become identical with some chunk of external reality? Bradley has a deep sympathy with this feeling, and consequently was unable to agree with Hegel that the real is simply the rational: indeed the thought horrified him. Thought and reality were for him too different. It is more than just rational thought that we identify with reality; it is the whole of the subjective life, of which thought is but one aspect. Bradley saw the real as experience, with all the diversity this entails. But experience is of a very different nature to plain thought. He was quite clear about this.

It may come from a failure in my metaphysics, or from a weakness of the flesh which continues to blind me, but the notion that existence could be the same as understanding strikes as cold and ghost-like as the dreariest materialism. That the glory of this world in the end is appearance leaves the world more glorious, if we feel it is a show of some fuller splendour; but the sensuous curtain is deception and a cheat, if it hides some colourless movement of atoms, some spectral woof of impalpable abstractions, or unearthly ballet of bloodless categories. Though dragged to such conclusions, we can not embrace them. Our principles may be true, but they are not reality. They no more *make* that Whole which commands our devotion, than some shredded dissection of human tatters *is* that warm and breathing beauty of flesh which our hearts found delightful. (*PL* 591)

His idealist colleagues, especially Bosanquet,[5] viewed this dissension from the Hegelian theory with horror. If reality is more than thought, it is other than thought. But this gap opens up the possibility of scepticism once again, this time within the Absolute—that is to say, within the very system that had been designed to exclude it; for the threat of Descartes's malicious demon was precisely what Hegel had attempted to remove. Further, they wondered if it could even be consistent to speak of a reality other than thought? Must it not be in thought for us to speak of it? Such statements looked to them, if not like a complete undoing of the Hegelian system, then certainly in tension with it.

---

[5] Bosanquet wrote a detailed commentary on Bradley's *Principles of Logic* (Bosanquet (1885*b*)), intended to bring him back into the Hegelian fold.

There can be no doubt that Bradley's worries place him in a predicament. On the one hand, he wants an identity between thought and reality, but, on the other, he is at the same time struck by the overwhelming difference between them both. How does Bradley get out of this dilemma? This is 'the great problem of the relation of Thought to Reality', which for him, he says, 'was long a main cause of perplexity and doubt' (*AR* 492). The problem is discussed and solved in chapter XV of *Appearance and Reality*. This crucial chapter, he says, 'contains the main thesis of this work' (*AR* 493).

He there accepts the basic Hegelian model, but modifies it almost beyond recognition, to fit in with his belief that reality is more than just thought. Is this not inconsistent? He readily admits that, 'If thought asserted the existence of any content which was not an actual or possible object of thought—certainly that assertion in my judgement would contradict itself.' But, he continues, 'the Other which I maintain, is not any such content' (*AR* 155). It is not anything that can be known, but still we know that it must exist. In order to understand this proposed solution we need first to grasp his view of the difference between thought and reality, and also his theory of judgement.

The real for Bradley is that which is particular or individual. It is substantial, in the sense of possessing a nature and existence independent of everything else. It is to be contrasted with that which is ideal, or belonging to the realm of ideas. But what is an idea? Bradley argues that, for the purposes of logic, an idea needs to be seen as a sign, something attributed to, or standing for, something else. As such it is no real object, but a mere symbolic content. This is most clearly seen in the fact that a single sign, such as a word or an expression, may be manifested in more than one spatio-temporal location, and hence in different objects. You or I may both utter or think the same word or expression. What makes them the same sign is their shared symbolic content. It is this content which we refer to the world, not the individual object in which it is found.

Content, moreover, is wholly general, a kind or type found in many instances, unlike reality, which is particular. Bradley's way of putting this is to say that everything real has both existence and content, or, as he alternatively expresses it, 'that' and 'what' (*AR* 143). In thinking or using ideas, we take some reality and abstract out its content, which we refer to some other part of reality. The problem is that the idea is merely an abstracted content, but reality—for instance, as it is given to us in feeling—is wholly individual and contains no abstractions, so it becomes hard to see how these abstractions can ever be true of, or identical with, the reality to which they are referred. As Bradley puts it, 'Ideas cannot qualify reality as reality is qualified immediately in feeling' (*ETR* 231).

Next we must look at judgement. In thought or judgement the thinking subject tries to put these ideas to some use. How does this work? We refer the abstracted content to some portion of reality and, through this conventionally established correlation, attempt to express something about the nature of reality. Or, as Bradley puts it, by returning the abstracted content back to reality, we aim to reunite the what and the that, provisionally estranged (*AR* 145). Let us consider an example, and, since every object has both existence and content, and is hence capable of acting as a vehicle of symbolism, let us take a physical rather than a psychological object. The red rose is a symbol of love. To form this symbol, we take the content of a red rose—what all red roses have in common—and decide by convention to refer it to that portion of reality which we call the phenomenon of love. One important point to note about this is that the judgement actually refers ideas to reality; it does not simply represent how they are referred to reality. This is significant and in fact requires a revision to the account just given. The content of the judgement is what we attribute to its referent; it does not itself contain any specification of that referent. The subject, as Bradley puts it, lies beyond or outside the judgement (*PL* 10, 41, 81). This means that, taking different judgements, we have no way of distinguishing their referents, hence they must all be taken to refer to the same thing, reality as a whole. All judgement then is of the form: reality is such that . . . where this is filled out by some content we attribute to reality (*PL* 630).

Our aim in judgement is to return ideas to their home—that is, accurately to match an abstracted and symbolizing content to its reality. However, at this stage a problem arises, for, since the subject of our judgement is that particular or substantial whole which is reality, and our ideas but an abstraction from that, they are never quite true of it. It is, for instance, wrong to attribute to reality the wholly abstract quality of being coloured, for being merely coloured holds nowhere of reality. Colour in reality requires, among other things, the existence of reflected light and some object which is coloured. Hence we must expand our attribution to include these aspects. But even to apply this wider predicate is no help, for that too is abstract, and thus not quite true of reality—there is, for instance, no light reflection without time, and there are no objects without spatial extension. In this way we set out on a process of continually expanding our judgements in order to make them true.

At this stage an objection might be raised. Is it not perverse to call the attribution of colour to reality 'false'? Of course, there are preconditions that must apply for it to be true. But, surely, something which is true on certain conditions is, if those conditions hold, true. Why should we suppose with Bradley that, for a judgement to be true, it must *include* its conditions of application within itself, by expansion of its predicate? Maclachlan[6] sees this as an extra and ungrounded assumption on Bradley's part.

In fact this is where Bradley's theory of truth really begins to work. Bradley believes that true thought is identical with the reality it is true of. But in that case, if the subject is 'wider' than the predicate we attribute to it, in order for the judgement to be true, the predicate must undergo expansion. Moreover, isolation or abstraction from context is, for Bradley, a distorting process, so that, just as a stone only becomes a paperweight when placed on a pile of papers, to call something 'P' in the context of Q is quite different from calling it 'P-in-the-context-of-Q'. Again the predicate must be widened. In so far as there is a difference between the two, we must modify the predicate until it fits reality. 'So long as anything remains outside, the judgement is imperfect' (*ETR* 233). We continue to do this until finally there is nothing in the subject not in the predicate. But completing this process leads to a startling result, for it is to make thought individual and particular like reality, to make it no longer an abstraction, but concrete reality itself.

An example may help here. Suppose that, using my symbol of the red rose, I attempt to represent the existence of love. Even if there is such a thing, my judgement will be false, for its subject is

[6] Maclachlan (1963).

reality as whole, and love, being but a limited abstraction from it, certainly does not characterize the whole. In order truly to characterize the whole, I need to add far more. Suppose that I do this and arrive finally at a long and complex description of everything, is my judgement now true? Still it seems not, for all I have is a set of ideas. But reality is more than a set of abstract generalities or ideas, however complex and all-embracing. Still more must be added. We must add all that is not thought; feeling, will, emotion, desire, in brief the whole world. Only now does our attribute truly and fully characterize reality as a whole, for it is identical with it. This last step, it must be noted, seems rather different in kind from those which precede it.

However, in this achievement—that is, in transcending abstraction—we have transcended thought, for the essence of thought is precisely to abstract. Once we add in the rest of feeling, we leave thought behind, for of these feelings—emotions, desires, and the like—Bradley asks, 'how in any sense can they be mere pieces of thought's heaven?' (*AR* 150). Thus, in the drive for truth, thought undermines its own existence and becomes reality. Just as a river loses itself into the sea, thought commits suicide by throwing itself into the Absolute (*AR* 153). The final product is beyond thought. Since thought is essentially abstract, all judgements are false. In order to be true they would have to cease to be abstract and thus to be judgements.

Since this prospect is but the limit of a continuous scale of lessening abstract content, there is perhaps a sense in which we may think of some thoughts or judgements as lying at this extreme. They are, we might say, completed or perfected thoughts, which, surviving the removal of all their abstract content, undergo a transformation from the ideal to the real or particular. If we allow this extension of the word, his theory might be usefully put by saying that true thoughts are of a fundamentally different nature from false ones. False thoughts are abstractions, true ones are concrete individuals. It is in this way that Bradley modifies Hegel's model to allow that only true thoughts are identical with reality.[7]

But, on a more standard understanding of thought, the quest for

[7] One interesting corollary of this theory is that, since this transformation can be more or less complete, room is opened up for a theory of degrees of truth and falsity, with the final consummation of thought taking the place of absolute truth. This will be discussed more fully in Chapter 7.

truth becomes a somewhat contradictory idea. The drive for truth is the drive to reunite existence and content, and this endeavour presupposes their separation. But its successful completion destroys this distinction, by annihilating the truth-bearer itself. The situation here is structurally the same as the fundamental contradiction of morality (*ES* 234–5) discussed in Chapter 1.[8] In achieving its goal of identifying the higher and lower will, morality undermines the condition for its possibility—namely, their separation. Likewise the search for truth is the attempt to unite existence and content, but, in achieving this, the preconditions of truth are lost. Thus describing our final product as 'truth' presupposes the story of how we got there. Yet, as one of his earliest critics put it, 'surely in all this there is something Quixotic. You cannot know the truth about anything without becoming everything, and you will be past *knowing* it then.'[9]

In this way then Bradley reconciles his apparently conflicting claims that reality is both one with, and different from, thought or truth. 'Truth, we thus can say, at once is and is not reality' (*ETR* 117). Thought is identical with reality, not as its whole nature, but as an aspect of it. But, even next to the rest of experience, thought as it stands is not identical with even a part of reality. It is only utterly transformed that it is able to reach its goal. Thus Bradley finds himself able to satisfy both his intuitive common sense—reality is not just thought—and his neo-Hegelian critics. To claim to have done this is no contradiction. 'Such anticipated self-transcendence *is* an Other; but to assert that Other is not a self-contradiction', for 'there is nothing foreign that thought wants in desiring to be a whole, to comprehend everything' (*AR* 160). It merely seeks to perfect itself, to complete fully what it tries to do. The point is just that, in doing this, it would be submerged and transformed into something quite other than thought. Nor, thinks Bradley, does this reintroduce an unacceptable level of scepticism into philosophy. For, although we cannot, of course, know or think what is beyond thought, the examination of thought itself and the demands that it makes shows us that there must be an other.

The departure from pure Hegelianism, it must be said, is both a strength and a weakness in Bradley's thought. It allows him to

---

[8] See p. 5.   [9] Ward (1894), 123.

abandon the implausibly extreme pure rationalism of Hegel, providing a place for feeling in a wider reality. On the other hand, he pays a strong sceptical price which at times introduces a rather mystical element into his thinking. For, although we can assert the existence of the Absolute, our comprehension of it is limited, because it is something beyond thought—it is an infinite and mysterious reality, of which we occasionally catch a glimpse, or feel a faint premonition, through the veil of our finitude and ignorance. But what is in no doubt is that these differences were quite enough to distinguish him from orthodox idealists who more or less slavishly followed Hegel, and make his philosophy highly interesting and original in its own right.

Almost no one, from his time to our own, has recognized that this was his theory of truth. Instead he has been claimed as a supporter by each of the three traditional theories of truth. To be charitable, we might say that this is because his real theory is rather strange and unusual, and because what he says bears some superficial similarities to other views. There is a measure of truth in this. We shall look at these erroneous interpretations because there are important lessons to be learnt from each, but in the end it is so plain that he cannot be said to hold any of these theories of truth, that we are forced to bring in factors external to the text from the history of Bradleian criticism to explain why these absurd stories persist.

2.12 *The Coherence Theory of Truth*

By far the greatest number of people have thought that Bradley held a coherence theory of truth[10]—that is to say, that he held truth to consist in the coherence of propositions among each other. The origin of this belief may be traced to Russell, who attacked the theory severely in a paper which, although explicitly directed against Joachim (who did hold such a view), made it clear that he believed this to be Bradley's view also.[11] This is still the popular opinion.

It is supported by the fact that a careless reading might well give

---

[10] e.g. Passmore (1966), 70; Wollheim (1969), 167–77; Haack (1978), 94–7; Grayling (1982), 132–4; Manser (1983), 106, 133; Blackburn (1984); Dancy (1985), 123–5.
[11] Russell (1906–7). The ostensible target was Joachim (1906).

this impression. But the real situation is quite otherwise. The fact
of the matter is that nowhere does Bradley say that truth *consists*
in coherence. For Bradley this is the *criterion*, not the nature, of
truth. He clearly states (*ETR* 202) that coherence is a *test* of truth.
On the other hand, it must be admitted that statements to the
effect that, the more coherent something is, the more true it is, are
ambiguous and not hard to misinterpret.

But even to say that Bradley used coherence as a criterion of
truth is to give a seriously inadequate account of his views. At no
point was Bradley concerned solely with the mutual coherence of
beliefs; equally important for him was their comprehensiveness.
The true set of beliefs must be both maximally coherent and
maximally comprehensive. Indeed, Bradley did not even see these
two as separate principles; for him they were but two complementary aspects of a single principle (*AR* 321). As will be seen
when we discuss his theory of contradiction, he believed that
contradictions were to be overcome and coherence obtained by
widening our view of reality—that is to say, by increasing comprehensiveness. Bradley takes coherence and comprehensiveness as
the criteria of truth, because he thinks that reality is coherent and
comprehensive, and thus that, the more coherent and comprehensive our theories are, the closer they are to being identical with
reality.[12] Just why he believes that reality is coherent and comprehensive we will show in our discussion below.

Is this a tenable criterion of truth? Most people have thought
not, for, even though they were designed to attack coherence as
a theory about the nature of truth, Russell's objections seem to
work against seeing it as a criterion also. Russell's primary objection was what might be called 'the Bishop Stubbs argument'. In
this argument it is supposed that we form a coherent and comprehensive set around the false proposition that Bishop Stubbs was
hanged for murder. But are we not obliged to call this set true? In
essence, the point is that there could be more than one comprehensive and coherent set, but presumably only one true one.

Bradley replies to Russell (*ETR* 213–14) that the statement that
Bishop Stubbs was hanged for murder is the product of mere
fancy, and we cannot let fancy in, because, if we let any fancy in,

---

[12] Degrees of truth are to be understood on the identity theory of truth, not as
degrees of identity, for that, of course, is an all or nothing affair, but as degrees
of similarity approaching closer and closer to identity.

we must let all fancy in. In other words, Russell has completely failed to understand the theory. Coherence and comprehensiveness are not the only criteria at work here. They need a source to work on, and this cannot be fancy. Rather, thinks Bradley, it is experience. In calling coherence and comprehensiveness the criteria of truth, Bradley means only that they are the critical tools used to assess and augment the base data of experience. Reality is given only in experience, but it is not given in a coherent and comprehensive form. Our task is to work the material of experience into such a coherent and comprehensive form. There is no knowledge independent of feeling, but no deliverance of feeling is infallible (*ETR* 203). All must be subjected to the test of coherence and comprehensiveness. If asked why we base everything in experience, Bradley can say only that he is no rationalist; he accepts this as a basic dogma of empiricism. Again we see that failure to grasp his doctrine of experience leads to misinterpretation of his system.

2.13   *The Correspondence Theory of Truth*

In his *Principles of Logic* Bradley seems to hold a correspondence theory of truth. He says:

A judgement, we assume naturally, says something about some fact or reality. . . . For consider; a judgement must be true or false, and its truth or falsehood can not lie in itself. They involve a reference to a something beyond. And this, about which or of which we judge, if it is not a fact, what else can it be? (*PL* 41)

There are several other references in that work to copying or corresponding (*PL* 41–2, 579–80, 583; cf. *ETR* 109 n.). This has led some to suppose that that was his theory of truth, if not always, then certainly at this period.

   It is quite clear that this was not his considered or favoured theory. In the second edition of the *Principles of Logic* he explains that he held it as a simplifying assumption only.

The attempt, made at times in this work for the sake of convenience . . . to identify reality with the series of facts, and truth with copying—was, I think, misjudged. It arose from my wish to limit the subject, and to avoid metaphysics, since, as is stated in the Preface, I was not prepared there to give a final answer. (*PL* 591 n.)

Elsewhere, in the *Essays on Truth and Reality*, he attacks the theory unmercifully. His objections to the correspondence theory of truth are twofold.

First, as we have already seen, he believes that thought and reality are so fundamentally different that any talk of correspondence between them is quite ridiculous. Thought is abstract and general, reality concrete and particular. But how can something essentially general ever correspond to something essentially particular? He objects that the one has been made external to the other (*ETR* 110), so that nothing can ever link them.

Secondly, he attacks the idea of bare unconceptualized facts to which truths are supposed to correspond. 'The merely given facts are', he says, 'the imaginary creatures of false theory. They are manufactured by a mind which abstracts one aspect of the concrete known whole, and sets this abstracted aspect out by itself as a real thing' (*ETR* 108). Bradley is appealing here to a thesis which can be traced in its origins back to Kant, and which, although it has met with variable fortunes over the years, enjoys current popularity in the slogan, 'All observation is theory-laden.' The claim is that we never experience reality as it is in itself, because all experience contains an element of our own conceptual input which goes well beyond the facts. To take a trivial example, I might seem to experience before me a glass, but, in characterizing my experience thus, I imply, for instance, that if I were to drop it it would break; but this involves an inference or theory (albeit low level) which goes well beyond my current data. Even if I were to deny the claim that all observation is theory-laden and argue that I am in direct and unmediated contact with reality, and hence in receipt of pure observational facts, the argument catches up with me. For they are only 'pure facts' relative to the theory of observation that I hold, and thus to call them this presupposes that theory. The lesson is that there is no such thing as pure observation. But, if there is no such thing as pure observation, there can be no infallible judgements of fact: as soon as they have enough content to state facts, our judgements become theory laden and therefore fallible (*ETR* 204).

One possible move from this position to a rejection of the correspondence theory is a verificationist one. If we never encounter such facts, what sense can it make to say that there are any? But, if there are no facts, there is nothing for thoughts to correspond to, and hence the theory collapses. Yet this is not Bradley's argument. He accepts that, below thought, in feeling, we do have access to unmodified facts. Therefore he objects to the correspondence theory, not because it implies the existence of such facts, but because it makes them inaccessible to thought. On his model of truth, thought must be given a path to truth, but, on the correspondence theory of truth, truth is quite inaccessible to thought.

In view of Bradley's objections to the idea, it might seem strange that he should have adopted correspondence at any stage of his career, even as a simplifying assumption. But really this is not so strange. Although ultimately opposed, until we meet the final distinction between thought and reality, the correspondence and identity theories of truth closely parallel each other. Up to a point they work in exactly the same way. In both theories the proposition must be worked on until it has everything the fact has. And, if we believed that there was but one great fact, this would mean one great proposition that tells everything exactly as it is.

At this stage there would still be a difference between them, in that one is a description and the other a fact. Wittgenstein's picture theory is an interesting comparison in this respect.[13] Most correspondence theorists are happy with this difference, but Wittgenstein was not. On his model we use not descriptions, but facts (things and relations), to stand for other facts (things and relations). Bradley would have seen this as a move in the right direction.

But still we have two things and not one. There are differences between them—most notably the modal difference that, because they are separate, they could exist one without the other. The final step for Bradley is to remove this last difference between them by identifying the truth-bearer with the truth-maker. Thus there is a sense in which the identity theory of truth is just the ultimate correspondence theory. In the *Principles of Logic* he does not commit himself to this last step, because it is metaphysical, and he wished to avoid metaphysics. In this sense the correspondence theory of truth is a perfectly sensible simplifying assumption for someone with an identity theory of truth. Thus it is somewhat misleading to say, with Candlish,[14] that the nature of truth was something about which Bradley changed his mind. The use of

---

[13] Wittgenstein (1961), 2.1–3.01.   [14] Candlish (1989), 335, 336–8.

correspondence as a pragmatic limitation is not inconsistent with a deeper commitment to the identity theory.

2.14   *The Pragmatic Theory of Truth*

Though few recent critics have claimed this, several of the early pragmatists believed that Bradley held a theory of truth which either placed him among their number, or at least brought him close to that position. And for many years one of the dominant subjects which filled the pages of *Mind* was an on-going debate between, on the one hand, Bradley, and, on the other, James, Schiller, and Sidgwick.[15] They all spent a great deal of time trying to show he was, or was becoming, or should become, a pragmatist. But, even if they failed in this, the debate served to highlight their differences, and thus assisted in the formulation of pragmatism. It is thus no exaggeration to say that in large part the modern theory of pragmatism was born in response to Bradley's philosophy.

On his side, Bradley never ceased to repudiate the pragmatic theory of truth, writing several sharp attacks on it. He made many criticisms of it. One of his main objections was that it was far from clear what the theory is really asserting. If we take it as the theory that truth is a question of success or admissibility in practice, how you understand this depends on how you understand the term 'practice'. If this is construed generously enough, then the theory is uncontroversially but trivially true, for success could even be success in corresponding to the facts. But, if this is understood more narrowly, then the theory seems incorrect, for surely a thing could be useful, but false. And herein lies Bradley's fundamental objection to the theory. He complains that it externally separates truth from knowledge and reality (*ETR* 110). Although it avoids the realist error of correspondence, through adopting utility as the standard of truth, it still thinks of truth as some kind of extra property which thoughts may or may not have. In taking truth as the identity between a thought and reality, Bradley sees it as an essential property of thoughts.

Why, if he was so clearly opposed to it, was Bradley thought

---

[15] For a discussion of *Mind* at this time, see Passmore (1976). For Bradley on the pragmatists, see *ETR*, chs. IV–V; *CE*, ch. XXXII. For the pragmatists on Bradley, see James (1893*a*; 1893*b*; 1910); Kenna (1966); Schiller (1903; 1907; 1908; 1910*a*; 1910*b*; 1913; 1915; 1917; 1925); Sidgwick (1894; 1904; 1905; 1908; 1909).

to be a pragmatist? This is not so strange a fact as might first be thought, for in many things he was in agreement with the pragmatists, and in others what he said bore a close, if in the end misleading, resemblance to their views. For instance, we have already noted (in Chapter 1) the pragmatic-sounding ring to his claim that truth must satisfy the intellect. The main difference, as we saw, is that, for Bradley, this is but one essential property of truth, and hence a criterion for it, not its defining essence. But even if he did not think that truth is satisfaction, he was thought by many to hold a coherence theory of truth, and this is closely related to pragmatism. Indeed, if we take pragmatism as defining truth in terms of our methods of reaching it, the coherence theory, concentrating as it does on the logical relations between statements, the examination of which is a very important method of determining truth, might even be thought of as a subspecies of it. But, as we have seen, this view makes the mistake of taking as a defining essence what was for Bradley but a criterion. Even so, his attack on the correspondence theory of truth, which takes thoughts to be true in so far as they copy or correspond to some external reality, was taken to be an attack on any form of realist or transcendent metaphysics, of the same kind as the pragmatists were engaged in. But even this is a mistake, for, as we have seen, despite its attack on correspondence, Bradley's theory remains at heart strongly realist. The final point of similarity lies in his claim that, for anything less than absolute truth, which, since absolute truth is beyond all thought, includes all thought, the criteria of assessment are all pragmatic. But even this is not pragmatism. Success, for Bradley, is a measure to use in the absence of absolute truth; it is not truth itself.

The real difference between Bradley's position and that of the pragmatists is that, for all these points of similarity, Bradley holds on to a higher absolute truth which is more than mere pragmatic value. Criteria of truth may be pragmatic, but truth itself is not. Of course, to a pragmatist, who operates with an essentially anti-realist view of the world, talk of absolute as opposed to lower truth, and talk of the nature of truth as opposed to the criteria of truth, are both nonsense. So, although Bradley thought of his position as different from pragmatism, the pragmatists had difficulty in seeing this. In their eyes he should have admitted that he was a pragmatist, it being words alone that held him back. But, since he did not accept their basic premiss, he could never accept that he was a pragmatist. Here the debate became at times rather confused, and circular.

2.2 THE LOGICAL STRUCTURE OF REALITY

We claimed in the section above that, for thought to become true or identical with reality, it had to undergo a massive transformation, for thought and reality are very different. In order to assess this claim we need to consider both. The nature of thought will be examined in Chapters 3 and 4, but let us spend the remainder of this chapter examining Bradley's view as to the fundamental nature of reality.

In the previous chapter we examined the claim that Bradley's philosophy was non-axiomatic—without basic foundations—and cast doubt on this. When we look closely at his thought, we see that the claim is not wholly true. There is an order of thought in his philosophy from certain more basic truths to others. These are as close as we come to axioms in his philosophy. Though not formally defining or exhausting the criterion, these are the basic things that ultimately satisfy the intellect, being such that, either logically or pragmatically, we simply cannot conceive them to be otherwise. These are the fundamental logical principles behind Bradley's philosophy. However, as we saw at the end of the last chapter, they could equally well be described as his fundamental metaphysical principles.

Bradley often speaks as if he had but one basic principle, that of non-contradiction. In *Appearance and Reality* he claims that he uses it as his only basis (*AR* 121). However, he gives a number of different accounts of it. Consider for instance:

Ultimate reality is such that it does not contradict itself. (*AR* 120)

The real is self-existent. And we may put this otherwise by saying, the real is what is individual. (*PL* 45)

There is, I contend, no criterion save that of system. (*PL* 685)

The Reality comes into knowledge, and, the more we know of anything, the more in one way is Reality present within us. (*AR* 489)

There is on each side an assertion, at least implicit, of the absolute truth that Reality must not contradict itself, and must, at least so far, be one.

And on each side the idea of system is used and accepted, at least tacitly, as the test of truth. (*PL* 681)

Although candidates other than non-contradiction have been suggested, it is hard to see how a single principle could be interpreted in so many ways. For instance, it is far from clear that all the negative arguments in *Appearance and Reality* really work in the same way.[16] Rather than looking for a single basic principle, a more fruitful approach is to see three or four interconnecting, inter-interpreting, and inter-supporting principles that form a basic core of Bradley's thought.

2.21 *Negation*

We can begin with Bradley's position on negation.[17] Bradley's theory of negation has two main components. First, he believes that propositions may be divided into two distinct classes, positive and negative. These stand at what he calls a different 'level of reflection' (*PL* 114) from one another. Positive assertions can sometimes be used without appeal to their negations, but negations must always be seen as the rejection of some prior positive proposition. This is not to say, as Ayer[18] took it, that all negative propositions must have been previously asserted or believed; rather, the precedence is logical—in saying that there is no tea in my cup I must be taken as denying the suggestion that there is. There is an asymmetry in our understanding. The reason why positive propositions may only *sometimes* be understood without appeal to their negations is that some positive propositions are in fact double negations, and thus at an even higher level of reflection.

The second aspect of his theory is a solution to what we might call 'the problem of negative facts'. This was discussed by Russell in *The Philosophy of Logical Atomism*.[19] The problem of negative facts can be put in a simple way. If propositions divide into two classes, positive and negative, and truth consists in some kind of correspondence to the facts, then it looks as if the facts also will divide into a positive and a negative class. But what is a negative fact? Surely talk of facts is just shorthand for talking about

---

[16] Airaksinen (1975), 14.
[17] For a good discussion of Bradley's view of negation, see Stock (1985).
[18] Ayer (1952).   [19] Russell (1956a), lecture III.

arrangements of things. Wittgenstein in his *Tractatus Logico-Philosophicus* says that 'What is the case—a fact—is the existence of states of affairs. A state of affairs (a state of things) is a combination of objects (things).'[20] But how can these be negative? I presented this difficulty through the notion of correspondence, but this was for convenience. You do not have to hold a correspondence theory to feel the force of this problem. The problem applies equally to Bradley with his identity theory. If it is impossible to compare a truth-bearer with a negative fact, it is surely just as difficult to identify one with such a fact.

Russell thought there must be negative facts, but Bradley will have none of this, and attacks the idea mercilessly.

If Not-A were solely the negation of A, it would be an assertion without a quality, and would be a denial without anything positive to serve as its ground. A something that is only not something else, is a relation that terminates in an impalpable void, a reflection thrown upon empty space. It is a mere nonentity which can not be real. (*PL* 123)

Bradley's way of avoiding this problem is to say that negative statements, such as that there is no tea in my cup, are not grounded in some negative fact of there being no tea in my cup, but in some positive incompatible fact—for instance, its being full of coffee. We do not assert this positive fact, for we may not know it, but none the less it is what grounds our statement. If a statement is true, there must be something in the world that makes it true. Thus the logical analysis and the metaphysical belief in the positive nature of reality are brought into harmony with each other.

But Bradley pays a price for preserving his basic metaphysical intuition. Negations are usually thought of as contradictory: a term and its negation can be neither true nor fail to be true together of something. However, a positive quality that excludes another is merely its contrary: they cannot both be true, but they could both fail to be true of something. For instance, it cannot be true that my cup is full of coffee and that it is full of tea, but these statements could both be false, for instance, if it is empty. Thus Bradley defines negation, not in terms of contradiction, but in terms of contrariety.

It might be thought that Bradley's answer is naïve, and that

---

[20] Wittgenstein (1961), 2–2.01.

there exist far better accounts of the semantics of negation, or the way in which negative statements are made true and false. According to the most popular view, famously expressed by Ayer,[21] every word divides the contents of the world into two classes, those things that it is true of (its range) and those things that it is false of (its complement). Sometimes the word has associated with it another, whose range is its complement and whose complement its range (e.g. coloured and colourless), but, if not, we can always invent one (Ayer invents the word 'eulb', whose range is the complement, and whose complement the range, of 'blue'), or, more simply, construct one by prefacing the word in question with the prefix 'not' or 'non' (e.g. blue and not-blue). It is then argued that, while the pair are negations of each other, which of them we call 'negative' is a purely pragmatic or contextual matter, and of no semantic significance. Placing the terms in statements, there is no special problem about what makes either of a pair of such statements true, since it is made true in precisely the same way as the other, which is to say in the same way as all statements.

But is this theory any real advance on Bradley's? It is usually claimed that it is, because, unlike Bradley's theory, this account preserves the idea that negations contradict each other, since, for example blue, is true of all that its negation, eulb, is false of (and vice versa). But, on closer examination, this turns out not to be the case. It is of the essence of this account that a statement and its negation are made true and false in exactly the same way as each other, but this creates a problem in cases of radical referential failure—that is, for statements of the form 'X is F', where the name or denoting expression 'X' does not refer to anything, and the speaker has in mind no alternative, more successful, means of identification. Whether they be thought of as false or lacking a truth-value, such statements are certainly not true. But this means that, where 'X' fails radically to refer, the two statements 'X is blue' and 'X is eulb' would both fail to express true statements. And, since pairs of statements are contrary when, if one is true the other is not, and contradictory when, both if one is true the other is not and if one is not true the other is, we see that blue and eulb are in fact contrary, not contradictory, terms. Thus, despite appearances, Bradley's and Ayer's theories are metaphysically on a

[21] Ayer (1952).

par. Both try to explain negation by the assertion of some positive quality which excludes, in Bradley's case by implicit reference to an unknown contrary and in Ayer's case by a disjunction of all contraries. Indeed, once we see this, there is a sense in which Bradley's theory is better, for do I really need to know the whole complement of any given property in order to assert its negation? Since both of these theories try to explain negation by means of exclusion or contrariety, they must therefore also explain this. We shall consider their explanations below.[22]

2.22   *Abstract Identity*

A second basic principle for Bradley is his opposition to identity statements, or more precisely to what in his time were called abstract identity statements. An abstract identity statement says that there is no difference between two things. It is to be contrasted with a statement of identity-in-difference, whose truth is compatible with the existence of a difference.

Bradley derived the criticism from Hegel,[23] who demanded that in all judgement there must be some difference or movement of thought. If we consider the form 'A is A', we must conclude, thinks Bradley, that 'It is no judgement at all. As Hegel tells us, it sins against the very form of judgement; for, while professing to say something, it really says nothing' (*PL* 141). Later, in the Appendix to *Appearance and Reality*, he again acknowledges the debt: 'Thought most certainly does not demand mere sameness, which to it would be nothing. A bare tautology (Hegel has taught us this, and I wish we could all learn it) is not even so much as a poor truth or a thin truth. It is not a truth in any way, in any sense, or at all' (*AR* 501). Bradley is quite clear that this could never satisfy the intellect. 'That abstract identity should satisfy the intellect . . . is wholly impossible' (*AR* 508; cf. *PL* 25, 371–2). Again he says, 'what then do we assert by AB = AB? It seems we must own that we do not assert anything. The judgement has been gutted and finally vanishes . . . In removing the difference of subject and predicate we have removed the whole judgement' (*PL*

---

[22] See §2.23.   [23] Hegel (1975), 165–8; (1929), ii. 37–43.

26). These are not, as Wollheim claims, false; rather they are not judgements at all.[24]

We are more familiar with this criticism through Wittgenstein's *Tractatus logico-philosophicus*. There he claims that, in a language composed solely of names and using a different name for each object, strictly there is no use for the identity sign.[25] 'A = A' does not provide us with any real information, either about the world or about our language. It does not actually say anything.

Wittgenstein's point concerns a very unusual language that asserts connections between names only. But it might be thought that Bradley is here rejecting all identity statements, not just those between names. This is how Wollheim takes him, and he then criticizes his view because there exist informative identities such as 'The morning star is the evening star'.[26] But this criticism is irrelevant, because Bradley is only attacking abstract identities, and to Bradley such statements are not abstract identities.[27] He makes a clear distinction between extension, what a term refers to, and intention, the meaning or sense of a term (*PL* 168–93), and, although the terms of such statements as 'The morning star is the evening star' do not differ in extension, they do differ in intention. Only where there is no difference in both intention and extension does Bradley think we should outlaw the statement. But this is rare. Few, if any, of the identity statements of ordinary language express abstract identities. Wollheim is therefore mistaken, and, with this understanding of the range of its application, we may accept Bradley's criticism of identity.

2.23 *Non-Contradiction*

Thirdly, we come to the principle of non-contradiction. This, too, is both a logical and a metaphysical principle. Just as Bradley cannot

---

[24] Wollheim (1969), 72. Two statements which provide apparent support for Wollheim's position are 'If you say that identical propositions are all false, I shall not contradict you' (*PL* 25), and 'If all propositions asserted mere identity, then every proposition would have to be false' (*PL* 371). But in general it is quite clear that Bradley thinks these 'senseless' (*PL* 25) or 'unmeaning' (*PL* 373). One possible explanation of his calling them false is that he is thinking here of absolute falsity, which is a kind of limiting position equivalent to nonsense (see Ch. 7).

[25] Wittgenstein (1961), 5.53–5.534.

[26] Wollheim (1969), 81–5.   [27] Maclachlan (1963), 157–8.

admit identity statements, he will not admit contradictory ones. Contradiction is usually described as the attempt to combine something and its negation. But, since Bradley takes an unusual understanding of negation, in terms of exclusion or contrariety, this results in a slightly different understanding than usual of what constitutes a contradiction. For him, two terms or statements are contradictory if they have nothing in common. The attempt to join two quite different things together with a mere 'and' is just contradiction.

> Things are self-contrary when, and just so far as, they appear as bare conjunctions, when in order to think them you would have to predicate differences without an internal ground of connection and distinction, when, in other words, you would have to unite diversities simply, and that means in the same point. This is what contradiction means, or I at least have been able to find no other meaning. (*AR* 505)

When viewed as a metaphysical rather than a logical principle, the prohibition on self-contradictory statements becomes the thesis that reality is such that it does not contradict itself.

There can be no question that this principle prejudices the case in favour of monism. A plurality of separate substances is ruled out as contradictory, because, if truly separate, they could not be united together in one universe. This fact in its turn raises interesting questions about the purpose of the arguments against relations. Rather than trying to prove a certain nature of reality, it seems their real aim is to demonstrate that our thinking can never quite match that reality. Given its significance, it is therefore crucial to see why Bradley puts forward this principle in this form. Why can we not conjoin two things with nothing in common?

He is commonly accused here of making an appeal to the principle of sufficient reason.[28] We cannot say that two things simply are joined, that there is a bare 'and', without being able to say how or why. This is sometimes taken to be but one instance of his general rationalistic view that we must be able to provide a reason or explanation for everything. But this cannot be correct, for there are many things that he admits we cannot explain, such as how the Absolute contains its appearances; it suffices to know that it can and it must. 'Not to know how a thing can be is no disproof of our knowing that it both must be and is' (*AR* 494).

---

[28] Campbell (1931), 25; Candlish (1984), sect. X.

More plausibly, sufficient reason may be taken as the claim that all truths are necessary.[29] Allard gives an explanation of this by saying that, for Bradley, all judgements are abbreviated arguments.[30] But to claim that all truths are necessary, or possess the necessitating force of valid arguments, is really little help, for at bottom it is not clear what is meant here by 'necessary'. To say that statements are necessary whose denials are a contradiction is no use, because it is precisely contradiction that we are trying to explain. But to read necessity as self-evidence is no help, for our question is precisely why Bradley found this requirement to be so intuitively obvious.

A quite different kind of explanation is that Bradley's principle is based on some kind of appeal to intuition or experience or imaginative conceivability. Broad claims that Bradley's opposition to separation depends on his belief that this is to abstract from prior unities, and that 'Unities are presented as such directly in sense-awareness or in feeling'.[31] Sprigge, in explaining Bradley's position, says, 'I have represented Bradley as concerned about the imaginability of the state of affairs described in relational propositions'.[32] There is some truth in this explanation. Bradley did, I think, have some kind of basic intuition about the nature of immediate experience. However, immediate experience is not common-sense experience, and not everyone has the same instinct as to what it is like,[33] so no appeal to intuition could ever have the force of an appeal to common sense. Thus, although he does partly rely on his intuitions, Bradley also thinks he can demonstrate the corresponding nature of feeling—in other words, that his intuition as to the nature of feeling can be fitted logically into his general schema. The nature of feeling both supports and is supported by the rest of his philosophy. This is not circular because his thought is not axiomatic, but evaluated largely in terms of its coherence.

The correct answer is that his formulation of the principle of non-contradiction is a consequence of his logical views. You cannot combine P and that which has nothing in common with P, for

---

[29] Russell (1906–7), 40; Russell (1910), 374.
[30] Allard (1984).   [31] Broad (1933), 86.   [32] Sprigge (1979), 167.
[33] Bradley, Russell, James, and Whitehead all emphasize the importance of immediate experience, but differ in their basic intuitions regarding its nature. See McHenry (1992), chs. 2–3.

the same reason you cannot combine P and not-P, because for Bradley not-P just means that which has nothing in common with P. Let us try to explain this. Since he does not accept pure negation, P and not-P must be read as P and something-else. This then raises the problem of how to distinguish contrariety from mere difference, how to distinguish a something-else that is contrary with, from a something-else that is merely different from, P.

One notable thing about pairs of contrary predicates is that they have in their ranges no common instances (for instance, nothing is both blue and green) while differences overlap (many things are both blue and square). This is the feature that Bradley uses to distinguish contrariety from mere difference. Not-P is for Bradley 'other than P' meaning 'wholly separate from P' or 'nothing in common with P'. So contradiction, which we understand as the attempt to unite some quality and its negation, and Bradley as the attempt to unite one thing with one of its contraries, is seen as the attempt to combine two things with nothing in common. Qualities with something in common (or, as Bradley expresses it, with some point in common) are merely different.

Whether or not they have anything in common may only come out on the wider picture. Some apparent contraries turn out to be simply differences. For instance, fast and slow may look contrary but are merely different because they may have the same speed in common. As we widen the picture, these notions are relativized. Thus we could only pronounce things to be contrary in the widest picture of all, for it is possible that, as we take a wider and wider view, apparent contraries, things that seem to have nothing in common, will turn out to have a common point, and thus be mere differences. This, of course, is what Bradley thinks will happen with all qualities, for in the very end there are no contraries. This is a purely formal limit, not in fact occupied by any pair of terms in the ultimate order of things.

Throughout the above I have spoken of contraries, but Bradley in fact uses the terms 'contrary' and 'contradictory' interchangeably. 'I do not find it necessary here to distinguish between these,' he says (*AR* 500). The explanation of this is that, if the reason why there can be no contraries is that there are no two things which cannot be true together, then this automatically rules out the existence of any contradictions as well.

Thus we see why Bradley thinks that two things with nothing

in common cannot be combined. It is his interpretation of the impossibility of combining P and not-P. It might be thought that this simply shows it to be a poor interpretation of P and not-P. While P and not-P cannot be combined, surely we *can* combine two things with nothing in common. That is to say, there are surely many predicates, which, although they in fact have no instances in common, nevertheless could have. This, according to the Bible, is the situation with the predicates man and being without sin, since no man is without sin. But these are not negations of each other, for unlike negations they *could* be combined. Absence of a common point, it seems, is necessary, but not sufficient to mark a term and its negation.

We might respond to this objection as follows. Taking P and 'nothing in common with P', it certainly seems as though we have to add an extra assumption here that these two not only are not but cannot be combined. But this is no different from the situation with the other standard theories of negation.

For what do P and not-P stand for, when they may truly be said of something? On Russell's view they stand for predicates which in the given case either are or are not instantiated. Let us call such cases respectively P-facts and N-facts. Now as things do actually stand there are no cases of a P-fact and its N-fact coexisting together, but now it is no longer clear why the world could not have both of these facts. This must be a further assumption. To be fair to Russell he is prepared to accept the relation of negation as basic—in other words, to accept that it is a brute fact about the universe that these exclude each other. Ayer, on the other hand, like Bradley, attempts to explain negation, so he does owe us an account. On Ayer's view, P and not-P stand for P and the complement of P (e.g. blue and eulb). These do not in fact apply to the same things, but, if they are of fundamentally the same kind, why cannot both of these be the case? Different properties could in fact divide the contents of the world into two, but, unlike contradictories, they do not necessarily do so. This must be a further assumption. So Ayer too has failed fully to explain negation.

All three accounts suffer from a common problem. So long as you call the two kinds of predicate 'P' and 'not-P', it seems obvious that they cannot be true of anything together. But once you try to spell this out, their incompatibility seems to be lost. You simply have two kinds of predicate which are not actually combined, but what we need is predicates that cannot be combined. None of these interpretations captures the modal point that negations cannot be combined. In this sense the views all seem to be on a par, and Bradley's is as reasonable or unreasonable as the others. But what it really shows is that we do not yet have an adequate understanding of negation.

This is perhaps the best place to discuss Bradley's relation to the famous Hegelian dialectic. Because of his understanding of not-P as some positive quality other than P, Bradley ends up by taking contradictories as really contraries, and this brings him closely into line with the Hegelian dialectic. The significance for a Hegelian of using contraries is that they may both be false, allowing us to open up a middle option which captures the best of both—the Hegelian synthesis of a thesis and its anti-thesis. Were they truly contradictory, no such middle ground would be possible, since the falsity of the one would entail the truth of the other and vice versa. Similarly, in Bradley's view, it remains possible that apparent contradictions may be overcome and on the wider picture be shown to be mere differences.

However, despite this similarity, Bradley's procedure is in one crucial respect very different from Hegel's. For Bradley, tensions are overcome by showing that they are not really in opposition at all—that is to say, by showing that the contradictions are all in our conceptions, and ultimate reality itself is wholly non-contradictory. Bradley was unable to accept Hegel's dictum of genuine and ineliminable contradictions at work within reality. For Hegel, 'Contradiction is the root of all movement and life', and he opposes the line of thinking whereby 'it is shifted into subjective reflection'.[34] But for Bradley, 'Ultimate reality is such that it does not contradict itself' (*AR* 120); rather it is 'the opposition between the real, in that fragmentary character in which the mind possesses it, and the true reality felt within the mind, [which] is the moving cause of that unrest which sets up the dialectical process' (*PL* 409). Bradley is perfectly aware that, by Hegelian standards, 'this doctrine is a heresy' (*PL* 410). Thus, for Bradley, dialectic is more a process of thought than a movement of reality itself. And, in so far as it is also a movement of reality, it leads to a wholly consistent goal. Bradley's Absolute is contradiction-free.

---

[34] Hegel (1929), ii. 67. This difference between Bradley and Hegel has also been noted by Findlay ((1958), 64) and Bedell ((1977), sect. 4).

One of the most notable things about Bradley's principle of non-contradiction is that he also uses it as a positive principle. This follows from his view of negation. The absence of contradiction, being a wholly negative property, must be based on some alternative positive feature. Bradley may seem to be begging the question when he associates this feature with the fundamental unity and integration of reality, but our analysis of the logical foundations of the principle of non-contradiction has shown that he is, in fact, quite justified in making this claim. The non-contradictory is the merely different, that which has a point in common and which is, in the wider picture, one. So non-contradiction is also a positive principle of individuality.

2.24 *Identity-in-Difference*

Non-contradiction and identity together form the two poles that propositions may not occupy, 'A = A' and 'A = B', abstract identity and complete difference. These limits give Bradley his final axiom: all genuinely satisfactory propositions should express a middle ground between these, an identity-in-difference.[35] To distinguish different from contradictory qualities, they must have a point in common, or belong to a wider whole. But they cannot be exactly the same, for then they would be identities, which are equally forbidden. So they must somehow express a union or synthesis of identity and difference. 'All judgements assert an identity in diversity and a diversity in identity' (*PL* 642). 'Every judgement makes a double affirmation, or a single affirmation which has two sides. It asserts a connection of different attributes, with an indirect reference to an identical subject; or it directly asserts the identity of the subject, with an implication of the difference of its attributes' (*PL* 174).

This notion can be given an innocuous interpretation: the same in one respect, but different in another. Yet this is not what Bradley means. He thinks it applicable to everything, including simple qualities, and these do not have the necessary complexity to support such multiple and differing resemblance relations. Nor does he think that this is merely a truth about propositions; it holds also

---

[35] See §§2.22, 2.23. This notion of identity-in-difference, which was of tremendous importance to the British idealists, derives from Hegel. 'Difference is therefore both itself and Identity. The two together constitute Difference' (Hegel (1929), ii. 44).

of the resemblance relations among objects, so that, as he strangely puts it, 'It takes two to make the same' (*PL* 141). To us this may seem plainly contradictory, but this is only so on our adherence to abstract identity and our view of contradiction. As we shall see in the next chapter, there is a sense in which Bradley too saw it as impossible, but that was not his ultimate view. In the end, for Bradley, his rejection of abstract identity and his view of contradiction make the doctrine perfectly consistent and, what is more, wholly inevitable.

At one stage Bradley claims that he does not find any principle of unity in diversity self-evident (*AR* 508). What he means is that there could exist one simple and self-identical object,[36] but that, if we accept the existence of diversity in the world, we are compelled also to see it as an identity. Diversity is an indubitable fact, it is given to us in experience. Without this, reality would be a single and undifferentiated atom. Thus Bradley finds it important to show that diversity is in fact given in experience.

It is this principle of identity-in-difference that lies behind his view of reality as a harmonious or organic system. Reality is the harmonious reconciliation of unity and diversity. The word 'organic', in common use among neo-Hegelians, is also supposed to suggest unity in diversity. An organism has many parts but, because they all work intimately together, it is also a single whole, in a way that the parts would not be were they simply lined up together.

With this we conclude our discussion of the fundamental nature of reality. Using one or other, or a combination, of these principles we can explain all Bradley's claims about the fundamental nature of reality. It is not clear that he sharply distinguished these principles. Bradley's claim that the nature of thought is quite incompatible with such a reality will be considered in the next chapter.

[36] This possibility is therefore not an objection to his theory, as supposed by Kulkarni (1957).

3

Subject and Predicate

IN the previous chapter we saw that thought, in aiming at truth or ultimate satisfaction, was, for Bradley, in fact aiming at an identity with reality. But, now that we have examined the fundamental nature of reality, it becomes harder than ever to see how this strange goal could be achieved. It was Bradley's view that, at the level of fundamental reality, diverse elements are at the same time identical. Yet how could our thoughts ever represent, let alone identify themselves with, such a situation? How, when we think of diversities, can we also think of them as identities? Bradley considers one possible answer:

The remedy might lie here. If the diversities were complementary aspects of a process of connexion and distinction, the process not being external to the elements or again a foreign compulsion of the intellect, but itself the intellect's own *proprius motus*, the case would be altered. Each aspect would of itself be a transition to the other aspect, a transition intrinsic and natural at once to itself and to the intellect. And the Whole would be a self-evident analysis and synthesis of the intellect itself by itself. . . . And if all that we find were in the end such a self-evident and self-complete whole, containing in itself as constituent processes the detail of the Universe, so far I see the intellect would receive satisfaction in full. (*AR* 507)

The suggestion under consideration here is in fact Hegel's view of the nature of thought,[1] and, although Bradley agrees that this would indeed provide an answer to the puzzle of how our thoughts could ever become identical with reality, he regrets that he is 'unable to verify a solution of this kind' (*AR* 507). The problem is that he is unable to accept that this idealized picture constitutes an accurate model of our actual thought. But not only does Bradley think that the nature of thought is quite unlike Hegel's model; he also considers it to be too unlike reality for thought and reality ever to be simply identified in the kind of way this model allows. Thus, as we saw in the last chapter, he finds himself obliged to

[1] See Hegel (1977). That it is Hegel he has in mind here is also supported by the footnote reference to McTaggart's *Studies in the Hegelian Dialectic*.

reject the standard Hegelian solution of the straightforward identity of thought and reality. Of course, as we also saw in that
chapter, he finds, in the postulation of a higher state beyond, but
incorporating, thought, a way in which they can in the end, and
in some sense, be identified. But, for the moment, let us draw back
from that final consummation, and look at his reasons for finding
thought and reality so different. We have already considered the
fundamental nature of reality. Let us therefore examine Bradley's
view of the nature of thought. Why is it so different from reality?

In the last chapter we expressed the difficulty by saying that
thought is abstract or universal, unlike reality which is concrete
and particular. Expressed like this, it is clear enough that there is
a difference, and often Bradley leaves the matter there. But we do
not yet have a clear enough idea of just what this difference consists in. Bradley's way of seeing the situation could be put like this.

In calling thought abstract or universal, he wishes to bring to
the fore the fact that it is essentially divisive. Thought works by
taking reality and carving off, or abstracting, some aspect from it.
For instance, the idea of blue abstracts, from the sea, its colour,
leaving behind its wetness and saltiness, while the idea of the sea
abstracts, from the waters of the earth, those of great magnitude,
leaving behind the rivers and the lakes. The abstracted aspect, or
idea, considered in isolation from its context, we then refer back
to reality. For instance, we look at the sky and judge that it is
blue, or look at a body of water and judge it to be the sea.
Selective in what it takes up and uses, thought thus divides itself
from reality. Moreover, there is with this process no limit to the
number of different aspects of reality that we can abstract, producing many different ideas. Thus thought also divides itself from
itself—that is to say, it is composed of a multitude of separate
ideas. We therefore see that with thought we bring division into
the world, and so thought takes an essentially pluralistic view of
the universe, where differences are divided from one another. But
reality, it will be remembered, although it manifests difference,
contains no division, being a unified or organic whole. Thus it is
clear to see that for Bradley no system of thought can ever be
identical with reality.

The consequence of this situation is that no thought in principle
can ever be wholly and ultimately true. Bradley tries to demonstrate this fact by showing that the pluralist or relational way of

thought is unavoidably subject to internal incoherence and self-contradiction. As such, he claims it could never be adequate, or true of reality. It is this attack that we shall consider over the next two chapters. It is perhaps worth adding at this point that Bradley is not here criticizing one kind of thought in favour of another; for in the argument above he has claimed that diversity marks the very essence of, and thus characterizes all kinds of, thought.

The pluralist view of the world is built on two closely connected foundations. On the one hand, there is the model of a thing, or subject, and its properties, and on the other hand, the model of relations connecting any two separate elements.[2] Bradley subjects both of these schemas to a series of devastating attacks. We shall look at his criticisms of the former in this chapter and his attack on the latter in the next chapter.

The subject–predicate schema is to be found in two separate but parallel forms—that is to say, as a thesis about the nature of our thought and as a thesis about the nature of reality. Bradley argues against both of these. We shall consider the two sets of arguments in turn, beginning with his attack on subject–predicate thought. As before, the general term, 'thought', may be replaced by the more specific, 'judgement'.[3]

3.1 SUBJECT AND PREDICATE GRAMMAR

3.11 *The Nature of Judgement*

Subject–predicate thought manifests itself in language as subject–predicate grammar, and hence it is that that Bradley directs his attention to. The orientation of Bradley's attack on subject–predicate grammar needs to be clearly understood, otherwise he may appear to be saying things which are in fact quite contrary to his real view. It will, therefore, be useful at this stage to give an overview of the objects, and the structure, of his attack.

We may begin by considering the subject–predicate form of judgement itself. According to a tradition that goes back at least as far as Aristotle, all significant judgements have a common form: they assert something (a predicate) of something else (a subject),

---

[2] See §4.24. Bradley does not believe in multi-place relations.
[3] See pp. 28–9.

while the two terms are connected together by some form of the verb to be (the copula). Thus in 'Aristotle is mistaken', 'Aristotle' is the subject, 'mistaken' the predicate, and 'is' the copula. Sometimes this form is less apparent and it requires analysis to bring it to the surface. Thus in 'Not everything which Aristotle said is mistaken', while 'mistaken' is once again the predicate, the subject must be read as 'some things which Aristotle said' and the copula as 'are not'. Although it may require work to bring this out, according to the view under consideration, all judgements do have this basic pattern.

Bradley is a fierce critic of this form of judgement. It is, he claims, internally incoherent and quite incapable of yielding true judgements about reality. In view of this opposition, we might be tempted to construe his argument as follows: thought is subject–predicate in form, this form is flawed, therefore thought is contradictory or false. Understood this way, he would appear to be condemning thought as inadequate to reach the truth, which would fit in with all that has been said so far.

To an extent this *is* what he is arguing. At other times, however, he seems to be arguing in a quite different way. This may be brought out by closer examination of the context of his criticisms. These occur in the *Principles of Logic*, as part of an attempt to justify his own rival theory of judgement against any competitors. According to his own theory, 'Judgment proper is the act which refers an ideal content (recognized as such) to a reality beyond the act' (*PL* 10), or, alternatively, 'a symbolic content referred away from its own existence' (*PL* 445). His claim is that, rather than being a composite whose parts relate one to another, the intentional content of a judgement forms only one idea which is attributed to reality as a whole. That is to say, all judgement involves but one idea, and all is referred back to but one logical subject, reality as a whole. Thus the judgement S is P in fact takes the logical form 'Reality is such that S is P' (*PL* 630).

This leads us to see his argument somewhat differently. Now we might represent him as arguing: if we used subject–predicate judgement then all our thoughts would be false, yet in fact we do not use it, rather judgement has a quite different structure. But this gives a quite different complexion to the matter, for now, rather than damning thought as a vehicle for truth, the purpose of the argument appears to be to attempt to rescue it.

In point of fact there is no real contradiction between these two ways of seeing Bradley's argument. Bradley does indeed wish to show that thought is inadequate to represent reality, but he is not interested in easy targets. The basic subject–predicate form he considers to be quite hopelessly wrong, but he does not think that it is the best we can do. Thus it is part of his aim to show that there are better forms of thought, immune to the most obvious objections against subject–predicate thinking. Nevertheless, it is his view that, even if we take the very best forms of thought, they too are found to be inescapably flawed. And here the attack on subject–predicate thought becomes relevant again, for the old problems catch up with us. Although they escape the most obvious criticisms of subject–predicate logic, it turns out that these higher forms of thought cannot escape them all. They suffer from the same basic flaw as subject–predicate ones. Therefore, an examination of the failings of subject–predicate thought remains central to understanding Bradley's view of thought in general, whatever form it may take.

3.12 *The Arguments*

Bradley has a number of objections to the subject–predicate model of judgement. But before we consider these we need to emphasize an important distinction that he makes between the grammatical and the logical structure of judgement. This distinction, which was innovative in Bradley's day, is, through the work of Russell and the philosophical tradition succeeding him, relatively familiar today. Its genesis is sometimes thought to lie with Frege, but, although Frege was one of the first to emphasize this, Russell in fact got the point from Bradley and consequently enshrined it in modern philosophy long before he encountered Frege.[4] This fact establishes an important continuity between Bradley's philosophy and that of his immediate successors.

The distinction is basically this. Relative to their different purposes, grammar and logic will analyse the same sentence differently in order to explain its working. For instance, a grammarian may be interested in tenses and genders, which the logician, without denying their presence, does not recognize as relevant to his

[4] Keen (1971), 8.

concerns. Instead he may note the presence of quantifiers and predicates, which the grammarian does not recognize as relevant to his interests. Grammar concerns individual languages or families of languages; logic concerns language in general as a vehicle of meaning and truth.

The distinction between logical and grammatical structure is significant because Bradley's arguments here are wholly concerned with the logical structure (or logical grammar) of judgements. He never denies that you can divide up grammatically most or even all judgements into a subject and a predicate, but this, he thinks, does not reflect anything about their true logical essence. That could never be subject–predicate in form. With this proviso in mind, let us now consider four of his arguments against the subject–predicate model of judgement.[5]

3.121 *Bradley's First Argument*

We can begin with one of his more minor arguments. This rests on the observation that often we use the same propositional schema when we are denying, doubting, or asking, as we do when we are judging or affirming. Take, for instance, the statement that 'The wolf is eating the lamb'. This may appear to be subject–predicate in form. But, if I may affirm this, I may just as easily deny, doubt, or ask exactly the same thing. But, reasons Bradley, if subject–predicate format is the essence, or as he puts it the *differentia*, of judgement, then it should not be found in cases of non-judgement as well (*PL* 13).

At first sight this argument seems very weak, but examining why this is so reveals an important and interesting difference between Bradley's approach to logic and that of modern logicians. A natural response to this argument is to say that, even if it is conceded that we can affirm, doubt, deny, or question one and the same statement, this does nothing to show that all judgements are *not* subject–predicate in form, just that they are not *uniquely* so. Perhaps subject–predicate form is something that is common to all these species of thought. This suggests the following kind of picture. The basic unit of meaning is to be thought of as a proposition,

---

[5] It will be noted that Wollheim's reconstruction of this argument (Wollheim (1969), 69–87) has not been included here. This reconstruction is a misrepresentation of Bradley's real views. See Griffin (1983) and Allard (1986).

where this is to be understood as an abstract object towards which we take various propositional attitudes, such as affirmation, but also including doubt, denial, and questioning.

Bradley approaches the matter from a wholly different angle. For him, the basic unit of meaning is the actual judgement, which is not to be thought of as broken up in this way into propositional content and attitude. This is why, as noted in Chapter 2, although for the most part they play the same role, it would be wrong simply to identify Bradley's notion of judgement with the modern notion of a proposition. Indeed, as his thought developed, Bradley became even more insistent about the difference between these two, explicitly rejecting the notion of an abstract meaning which is not somehow put to use, something which is implicit in the idea of a proposition. Ideas do not 'float' and must always be tied down to some specific task; for it is of the essence of a symbol that it actually refers to something.[6]

3.122   *Bradley's Second Argument*

To say simply that thought is subject–predicate in form is not the most helpful of statements, for the nature of the relationship between a subject and its predicate is not itself a clear matter. Thus advocates of the theory owe us an explanation of this basic relation. This they have often attempted to provide. A second kind of argument employed by Bradley against subject–predicate judgement consists in attacking the various explanations of this that were current in his day, with the aim of showing that none is satisfactory. This is, of course, a wholly negative style of argument, and thus incapable of proving that no satisfactory account is possible. But when the most obvious and only available candidates for explanation have been dismissed, the prospects of any coherent interpretation must seem severely handicapped. There are three views that he considers.

The first theory is that of class-inclusion. On this model, to say that 'A is B' is to claim that A belongs to the class of B-things. For instance, the statement that 'Bradley is a Hegelian' places Bradley in the set of all Hegelians. Bradley's objection to this theory is that it is not well able to deal with attributions of uniqueness. It is, he suggests, absurd to suppose that, in making the judgements 'It

[6] See pp. 143–4.

is our son John', or 'It is my best coat', or '9 = 7 + 2', I think of
a class of 'our sons John' or 'my best coats' or 'things equal to
7 + 2', for no such classes exist (*PL* 21). This must be considered
a weak argument. There is no reason to demand that in such cases
the class in question need have more than one member.

A more serious objection, which Bradley does not raise, would
be that the theory offers us very little by way of explanation.
What is the class of all B-things, except the class of objects with
the property B? But this is precisely what we are trying to explain.
Introducing classes here adds extra ontological commitments for
little explanatory gain.

The second theory which he considers is that of subject-
inclusion. On this model, to say that 'A is B' is to say that B
belongs to or is included in the subject A. Thus now the statement
'Bradley is a Hegelian' would claim that the property of being a
Hegelian belongs to the subject we call Bradley, that it is included
in the class or set of properties which together make up Bradley.
Here it must be admitted that the sets introduced do more work,
taking over the functions of a subject term. And if it is thought
that the notion of a set of properties is clearer than that of a
subject in which they inhere, then some explanatory advantage
would seem to have been obtained. However, Bradley cannot accept
this answer either. He objects that this model lacks any non-
arbitrary way of dealing with relational judgements, such as 'A is
simultaneous with B'. We could construe this as saying that 'simultaneity with B' is to be found in A. But equally we could
construe it as saying that 'simultaneity with A' is to be found in
B, or as saying that 'simultaneity' is to be found in the pair A, B.
Each of these requires us to torture the material into one shape or
another, but, claims Bradley, 'if torture is admitted, the enquiry
will become a mere struggle between torturers' (*PL* 22). He also
objects[7] that a mere set of abstract qualities is unable to capture
either the unity or the particularity of objects.

The third model considered is that of subject–predicate identity.
The theory he has in mind here is Jevons's equational logic,[8] which
enjoyed considerable popularity at the time, and he spends an
accordingly greater time discussing it (*PL* 22–6, 27, 370–88). On
this theory, to say that 'A is B' is literally to identify A and B as
one and the same thing, and to be read 'A = B'. Bradley is quick

---

[7] See pp. 77–8.　　　　[8] Jevons (1879), ch. III.

to point out that, despite the equal sign and the name 'equational logic', the relation here is not equality of amount but actual numerical identity. Whatever is picked out by the left-hand side of the equation is supposed to be literally identical with whatever is picked out by the right-hand side.

Bradley begins his critique of this theory by noting that much of its plausibility derives from careless formulations of the equations in question. For instance, if the judgement 'some men are negroes' is read as the equation 'some men = negroes' then, strictly speaking, it is false, for, while some men are, some men are not, negroes. In order to state a truth the left-hand side must be made more precise, so the equation reads 'negro men = negroes'.

Once this is done, he thinks that the failing of the theory becomes all too obvious. This is simply that the judgement says nothing, but is merely an empty expression of abstract identity. It is a tautology, but, as we saw in the last chapter, since he rejects all such tautologies, this in effect means that it is no judgement at all. In the process of making it fit the theory, 'The judgement has been gutted and finally vanishes. . . . In removing the difference of subject and predicate we have removed the whole judgement' (*PL* 26). Thus, in the final analysis, Jevons's theory renders judgement itself impossible.

Thus this model is quite inadequate as an account of how we think. In view of the magnitude of its failings, it might seem a wholly worthless theory. But to leave the matter there would be quite misleading, for, although it may be false, Bradley reserves for its author, Jevons, a level of praise, among the highest in all of his works (*PL* 386–8). Why is this? The reason is that he thinks the theory, despite its shortcomings, has captured one very important truth. Even if they are more than just identities, he thinks that Jevons is correct in saying that all judgements must involve identity: 'an identity must underlie every judgement' (*PL* 28). To Bradley, this is a necessary truth about all judgement, for, as we saw in the previous chapter, he could not accept any union of mere differences.

3.123 *Bradley's Third Argument*

With Bradley's third argument against subject–predicate thought we enter a new higher level of insight and persuasiveness. However, in order fully to appreciate it, we first need to look again at his theory of meaning or ideas, already briefly discussed at the end of the last chapter. The best way to understand this theory is to examine the context of its origin—that is to say, the opposition against which it was first developed. At the time when Bradley began to write, the prevailing view of meaning was the empiricist theory, whose essence and origin can be traced back to Locke. According to that view, meanings are ideas, which in their turn are psychological entities that copy and thereby represent reality. They could be thought of as mental images or, to put it at its most basic, pictures in the head. Conceived of as very similar to perceptions, and distinguished from them by a lesser degree of vivacity, these psychological entities were thought to belong to fundamentally the same species as sensations or emotions. Their study is thus a branch of what today we would call psychology. Hence this kind of a view of thought is often called psychologism.

Like the German logician Frege, who simultaneously developed similar ideas,[9] Bradley had no sympathies of any kind with this approach, and began his *Principles of Logic* by launching into a vehement attack on it. 'In England', he says, 'we have lived too long in the psychological attitude . . . we have as good as forgotten the way in which logic uses ideas. . . . For logical purposes ideas are symbols, and they are nothing but symbols' (*PL* 2–3). What did he mean by this? There were at least two points to his attack.

His first point can be explained like this. Sensations and emotions are objects, they are real and they have a nature. As Bradley puts it, they possess both 'that' and 'what', existence and content. Ideas also have these two aspects but, he argues, they have a third as well, and it is in this only that their significance for logic is to be found. The third aspect is their meaning: ideas symbolize or stand for something else; as Bradley expresses it, they refer away from themselves. Anything can do this, but not everything does, and nothing must. That is to say, there are no special properties that make things refer, it is simply a question of how they are used. This is shown by his example of the language of flowers. We use a red rose to symbolize love, but we could have used any other flower and had the rose stand for something else, or again we might not have used it to stand for anything. The fact that we think of ideas as images tends to obscure this, so there is a tendency

---

[9] Frege (1980), 126–7.

to conflate meaning and content. But nothing is intrinsically a symbol. It is only a symbol when it acquires the third aspect, its meaning. By way of illustration, the difference between a symbol and a fact can be thought of as like the difference between a painting and an accidental spillage of paint on to a canvas.

We arrive at Bradley's second point if we ask, what is it that we refer away to reality? This is not easy to answer precisely, but one thing that it certainly is not is a psychological image or fact. Even if it employs such a psychical image, the judgement that whales are mammals does not qualify whales with mammal images (for these are elements of human psychology). It is the meaning of the idea, not the idea itself, that we attribute to reality. This is something we abstract from the existence of the image. It does not exist as a concrete individual. It is a universal. To take an example, it is not this mental image or this particular flower that refers to, for example, love, but any image or flower of this class. Yet there is only one symbol here. Otherwise how could two people have the same idea, or one person the same idea for more than a second? By way of illustration an analogous confusion might be to suppose that, for example, an oil-painting of some object is saying that that thing is a canvas covered in oil pigments. It is not the picture itself, but what it depicts, that we attribute to reality.

Putting these two points together, we arrive at Bradley's definition of a logical idea or sign. He says, 'A sign is any fact that has meaning, and meaning consists of a part of the content (original or acquired), cut off, fixed by the mind, and considered apart from the existence of the sign' (*PL* 4).[10]

We can now turn to see how he utilizes this view of ideas in one of his arguments against subject–predicate judgement. He argues that thinking of ideas as entities in the head can lead to confusions about the logical structure of judgement. We may, for instance, consider our judgement that 'The wolf is eating the lamb'. This might appear to be a complex of ideas connected together in subject–predicate form. But before we conclude that this is indeed the case, we need to make an important distinction between, on the one hand, connections between symbols, and, on the other

[10] In a footnote to the second edition of the *Principles of Logic* Bradley modifies this definition slightly. In particular he rejects the implication that a sign could exist 'cut off' from the world, or apart from its use in a judgement. For a further discussion of this rejection of 'floating ideas', see pp. 143–4.

hand, symbolized connections. Again this is most clearly seen by an example of a picture. In order to depict a tree on top of a hill you must place some paint on the canvas adjacent to the paint which already represents the hill. If you place the new paint on top of the old mark, you will in fact depict a tree in front of a hill. The physical connection of adjacency between the two symbols is itself a symbol, and differs from the connection it symbolizes (standing on top of), just as much as the two patches of paint differ from what they symbolize (the tree and the hill).

If we return to our judgement, claims Bradley, we see that the distinctions and connections we find among its components are all of the second kind. 'Eating' is simply a third idea alongside 'wolf' and 'lamb'. It symbolizes the connection between the wolf and the lamb, but does not itself make any connection; it does not connect the ideas, and it certainly does not connect the wolf and the lamb themselves. That it does not actually make a connection between the ideas is seen from the fact that the same set of ideas also symbolizes 'the lamb eats the wolf'. To put the point in Bradley's own words, 'The relations between the ideas are themselves ideal. They are not the psychical relations of mental facts. They do not exist between the symbols, but hold in the symbolized. They are part of the meaning and not of the existence' (*PL* 11).

Clearly what actually connects the symbols is their order. But, and this is the important point, what connects the symbols is of no concern to logic. Logic is concerned only with logical ideas or meanings, and not with what, in physical reality, happen to be their vehicles. To make the analogous point in terms of art, we might say that the techniques of painting some picture do not concern someone whose sole interest in the picture is in what it is a picture of.

Finally, argues Bradley, if we concentrate only on what is symbolized, we see that the whole judgement is on a par. In terms of meaning there is no reason to separate out any one bit from any other. In symbolic terms the whole judgement is homogeneous and one idea, or at least any divisions within it are arbitrary. Thus he claims that whatever exists before the mind is one idea, not a subject–predicate complex. Bradley himself puts the point this way: 'The whole in which they subsist is ideal, and so one idea' (*PL* 11). By analogy we might say that, although in terms of painting technique you may divide up a picture how you like, for the purposes of representation, such divisions are arbitrary, so any picture is symbolically homogeneous and thus one.

3.124 Bradley's Fourth Argument

In order to understand Bradley's next argument, we need to consider another feature of his theory of ideas that we did not mention above. We have already seen that meaning or logical symbolism is effected, not through particular objects or ideas, but through abstract or universal meanings, however, Bradley believes that symbolism is general, not just in itself, but also in its signification, referring not to particulars but always to kinds or classes. Thus meaning, as one commentator has put it, runs not only from a class, but also to a class.[11]

The fourth of Bradley's arguments against subject–predicate logic that we shall consider is somewhat more extended, occupying most of chapter II of the *Principles of Logic*. It begins by considering our pre-philosophical common-sense assumption that judgement says something about some fact or reality, that it points away from itself to something in the world. This Bradley expresses as the claim that it is categorical in nature. This may seem unproblematically obvious, but at this stage he brings into consideration the claim introduced above that all symbolism is general and not particular in its signification. This leads him to be most impressed by an argument derived from Herbart, to the effect that, if judgement consists in the union of ideas, and all ideas are general, then all judgement must be hypothetical, and not categorical at all. But this directly contradicts our belief that judgement tells us about how things are in the world.

According to Herbart's argument,[12] 'If judgement is the synthesis of two ideas, then truth consists in the junction of unreals' (*PL* 46). A sentence like 'All whales are mammals' links universals, and can only mean 'anything of the whale kind is of the mammal kind', making no reference to anything specific. But this tells us nothing about reality, unless we assume also that these general properties are instantiated, so that it would be better represented as saying, 'If anything is of the whale kind it is of the mammal kind.' In other words, it gives us, not specific details about how things are, but merely generalized information about how things

[11] Wollheim (1969), 31.   [12] Herbart (1850–93), i. 91–4.

would be if certain other things were the case. Herbart's argument applies to all judgements. Not even apparently singular judgements can escape.

But this result directly contradicts our intuition that judgement can give us definite information about how things are in the world. Bradley is sympathetic enough to this intuition to wish to reject the conclusion, but, finding no error in the structure of Herbart's argument, his only option is to question its premisses. And this he does. 'The conclusion, thus urged upon us by Herbart, follows, I think, irresistibly from the premisses. But the premisses are not valid' (*PL* 44). Herbart makes only two premisses. The first, that ideas are general not particular, we have already seen that Bradley accepts. He thus finds himself rejecting the second, that judgement consists in the union of discrete ideas, that is to say, that it has a subject–predicate structure. Herbart's argument thus constitutes a fourth reason for rejecting the subject–predicate analysis of thought. Instead, Bradley claims, judgement consists in the application of a single ideal content to reality as a whole.

Since this is not the only response possible to Herbart's argument, the plausibility of Bradley's answer clearly depends upon the strength of his reasons for not rejecting Herbart's first premiss, that is, on his reasons for accepting the generality of all symbolism. He therefore spends a great deal of time defending this doctrine. He remains quite committed to the thesis: 'Nothing in the world that you can do to ideas, no possible torture will get out of them an assertion that is not universal' (*PL* 63). Let us consider whether he is successful in establishing this. No one, of course, would wish to deny that many ideas are general, but there seem to be some obvious counter-examples. These are names, demonstratives, indexicals, and definite descriptions. Is Bradley correct in his insistence that, despite appearances, these too are general? We will consider each of them in turn.

3.1241 *Proper Names*

It is a popular belief that names, such as Oxford, Hegel, or UNESCO, pick out, not general types, but the individuals whose names they are, and moreover that they do so, not by describing some general type which has but one instance (for example, being a medieval university town inside a twenty-four-and-a-half-kilometre ring road), but simply by standing for or latching on to the individual object in question. This view of names, associated in our century with Russell's logically proper names, Wittgenstein's names for simple objects, or Kripke's causal theory of names, constituted the orthodox opinion in Bradley's own time as well, due to the dominant influence of Mill.[13] Mill expressed this idea by saying that names had denotation but no connotation. Bradley, on the other hand, is quite contemptuous of this suggestion. Part of the cause of this contempt is admittedly a verbal confusion which causes undue irritation to Bradley. Mill's view is sometimes expressed by saying that a proper name '*stands* for something but does not *mean* anything' (*PL* 59), but for Bradley this is just what meaning is—to stand for something.

Yet Mill's thesis can be put in a way that allows the real difference of opinion to be clearly seen, and that is this. According to Mill's view, although a name means or stands for something particular, it is not a description or general characterization of, but a mere mark for, or pointer towards, some individual object. But this is something that Bradley cannot accept. If the claim is that a name, John, 'is the ideal counterpart to pointing in particular to John, then you must allow me to doubt if you comprehend what you are saying' (*PL* 60) he says. Why does he think this? He gives two arguments.

Part of his worry is that he does not see how, or by what mechanism, an idea can refer, except by some thing's answering to its ideal content. 'That very process, which makes it a sign and associates it firmly with the thing it signifies, must associate with it also some qualities and characters of that which it stands for. If it did not to some extent get to *mean* the thing, it could never get to *stand* for it' (*PL* 60). If you take away its descriptive character, what connection remains between an idea and its object? In criticism of this argument, although the connection between referring item and referent is certainly something that needs explaining, it is far from clear why answering a description should be the only way of being a referent. Kripke, for instance, explains the connection as a conventional correlation, established through an initial baptism and then passed down a historical chain of speakers, each of whom intends to use the word in the same way.[14]

---

[13] Russell (1956a), 201; Wittgenstein (1961); Kripke (1980); Mill (1872), ch. 2.
[14] Kripke (1980).

Bradley's second worry is that, if numerous people use a word to refer to the same thing, they must surely have more or less the same idea in mind. If we could all have different ideas or even no idea, how would we know that we all mean the same? Now, it is certainly true that, if names had associated with them no descriptive content whatsoever, it is hard to see how two people could ever find out whether they agreed or disagreed in their use of a particular name, except by pointing to the object they were referring to, which, of course, for a great many names is not possible, and even where it is possible may be ambiguous. Kripke, however, has argued that, if names do have descriptions associated with them, it is possible to see these as merely fixing the reference of the name not giving its meaning. That is to say, we may think of them as simply beliefs that we hold about the bearer of the name with which they are associated. They do not give its meaning because the reference of the name remains unaffected, even if we change these beliefs.[15] I may, for instance, change from thinking of John Major as a man who deliberates slowly and carefully to thinking of him as someone who simply cannot make up his mind, but I am still thinking of the same person. This argument would allow us to dismiss Bradley's second reason for denying that proper names cannot be particular.

3.1242 *Demonstratives and Indexicals*

Even if we granted him his point, it might be thought that, if not names, then at least demonstratives or indexicals, like 'this', 'that', 'here', 'now', and 'mine', are able to do the required task. But, echoing Hegel's discussion of Sense-Certainty in the *Phenomenology of Spirit*,[16] Bradley thinks that such expressions are no less universal than names, and thus quite unable to pick out individual objects. Of course, he is not ignorant of the fact that they are often thought able to do so, and he argues against this thesis in at least three different ways. The arguments centre around the paradigm example of a demonstrative, the word 'this'.

He begins in the *Principles of Logic* by claiming that there are two different ways in which the demonstrative 'this' may be used— that is, two different ways in which things may present themselves to us. The difference he marks terminologically by what he calls

---

[15] Ibid.   [16] Hegel (1977), ch. 1.

'this' and 'thisness'. By the latter he means essentially the spatio-
temporal individuation of some object. This provides a sense of
exclusion, a sense in which we have before us some one thing and
not another, but only in virtue of that object's place within a
series. But, he claims, different series may arrange the same things
differently, so that the object 'does not exclude except in *this*
sphere' (*PL* 64). That is to say, things thus distinguished seem
unique only because of the particular point of view from which we
consider them, because of the individual co-ordinate system within
which we happen to locate them. But 'such particularity in space
or time, such an exclusive nature, after all, is only a *general*
character . . . It marks the sort but it misses the thing' (*PL* 66).

On the other hand, 'Beside the idea of exclusion in a series,
which is mere thisness, we have also the idea of my immediate
sensible relation to reality . . . we have "this"', (*PL* 67). My immediate sensible relation to reality does latch on to something
exclusive and unique, but, claims Bradley, it is not a quality of the
given or part of its content. 'It is unique, not because it has a
certain character, but because it *is given*' (*PL* 64). Why is this fact
of givenness so different from the fact of thisness? Bradley's idea
is that, although we can form something like an idea of givenness,
unlike our idea of thisness, that idea can never be used as a symbol in judgement. Bradley's reason for saying this is highly confused. He thinks that we cannot use our idea of givenness to refer
to anything, because that idea is unique, and hence so must its
referent be, but this would be to imply two incompatible uniques.
Quite what the incompatibility that Bradley sees here consists in
is not made very clear.

When the subject is taken up again in *Appearance and Reality*,
the argument is simplified. Rather than saying that we have an
idea of 'this' but that we cannot use it, it is now claimed that we
cannot form any idea of 'this' at all. He argues that, whenever we
are inclined to describe something as 'this' or 'mine', these terms
may be taken in either a positive or a negative sense. The positive
sense applies to a realm below distinctions, where the what and
the that are identified—that is to say, to a felt reality, prior to all
conceptualization. In this respect, although finite, it is like the
Absolute itself. It does not, however, act in an exclusive way, and
can be absorbed into the wider reality of the Absolute. But when
we try to capture this feeling in thought, we produce only a negative

sense of 'this', which, although it is exclusive in character, is, by virtue of being an idea, already inconsistent with itself and suffering reference beyond itself—it is 'this' as opposed to 'that'. But, in that case, its sense of repulsion, just like the sense of repulsion associated with thisness, is relative and holds merely within one whole (*AR* 201). So, as was the case with 'thisness', the negative sense of 'this' or 'mine' turns out to be a merely general characteristic, and something quite capable of being absorbed within a wider reality.

In the second half of the relevant chapter of *Appearance and Reality* the case is made in yet another way. 'This', it is claimed, has no content that is uniquely its own: it can refer to anything. But, if it can refer to anything, it is general. The same point is also made in the *Principles of Logic*. This, here, now, and I might seem to pick out individuals, but, because they can apply to everything, they are really just universals (*PL* 49, 63), for they can apply to any object. Everything is this, every place here, every time now, and every person I. Indeed, because they can apply to anything, they are, for Bradley, the most general kinds of expression possible. Thus Bradley argues that, despite whatever it may seem to us, demonstratives and indexicals are of no use in picking out individuals, they are entirely general.

3.1243 *Definite Descriptions*

The arguments against demonstratives and indexicals are no more successful than those against names. But, as before, even if they were successful, there would remain a further line of defence. Could individual objects not be picked out by definite descriptions? Does, for instance, the expression 'a medieval university town inside a twenty-four-and-a-half-kilometre ring road' not uniquely pick out Oxford? It is clear that many definite descriptions are ambiguous, relying on context, to effect their unique reference, but suppose the descriptions were, or were made, specific enough, might they not secure singular reference? Bradley is unconvinced by this suggestion, for he argues that no matter how we express them they could always refer to something else—that is to say, it is always logically possible that there might exist more than one object answering to the description, and as such the descriptions must be general. He says, 'our terms are all general,

and state a truth which may apply as well to many other cases'
(*PL* 49), and again 'The event you describe is a single occurrence,
but what you say of it will do just as well for any number of
events, imaginary or real' (*PL* 63). It will not do to object that
there might *in fact* be only one object that answered the description, because, for Bradley, there is in the end no ultimate difference between real and imaginary objects of reference.[17]

With this conclusion, for Bradley, the thesis of the generality of all
symbolism is established. He takes it that from this it also follows
that, if there is to be any categorical judgement at all, thought may
not consist in the union of any subject and predicate. Thus with
this argument Bradley's case against subject–predicate grammar is
complete.

3.13   A Common Objection

We may conclude our discussion of Bradley's rejection of subject–
predicate propositions by considering an objection to his thought,
made initially by Russell, but commonly repeated since that time.
In view of the arguments just considered, this objection will seem
strange, for it is that Bradley attempted to reduce relations to
properties because he only accepted subject–predicate grammar,
and that this was his undoing. Why did Russell say this?
   The accusation first occurs in Russell's *Principles of Mathematics*.[18] He there claims that it is Bradley's belief (held perhaps
unconsciously) that all propositions ultimately consist of a subject
and a predicate, and that this leads him to adopt what Russell
calls the monistic theory of relations. For any proposition which
we might characterize by the form aRb, this theory regards the
relation as a property of the whole composed of a and b, and thus
equivalent to, and more accurately expressed by, a proposition of
the form $(ab)R$. Russell objects to this theory on the grounds that
it cannot deal with asymmetrical relations. It cannot, for instance,
distinguish between 'a is greater than b' and 'b is greater than a',
expressing both by the common propositional schema, (ab)

---

[17] This is because he rejects 'floating ideas'. See pp. 142–5.
[18] Russell (1903), sect. 212. See also Pears (1967), 165.

greater than. The correct response, claims Russell, is to deny that all relations are subject–predicate in form and to accept relational propositions as a separate and irreducible type.

Russell makes the accusation because this is how he understands the foundation of Bradley's theory of judgement, that in judgement we ascribe a predicate to the whole of reality. But unfortunately he has misunderstood that theory. This can be seen by the fact that Bradley has an easy response to the objection from asymmetrical relations. What is transformed into a predicate is not just the relation, which is symmetrical, but the whole relational situation, which is asymmetrical. The predicate is not 'being greater than', but '*a* being greater than *b*', and this is attributed, not to the set (*ab*), but to reality as a whole.[19] The full relational situation is attributed to reality as a whole. Russell has only a limited grasp of Bradley's theory; he sees it as a redistribution of subject and predicate roles within a proposition, whereas in fact Bradley is taking the whole proposition to be one predicate, whose ultimate subject is reality itself. Thus, rather than forcing all propositions to display a subject–predicate form among their parts, Bradley is demonstrating that in truth none of them has this form.

Thus, for the purposes that he wants to employ it, Russell's claim is wholly spurious. In another sense, however, it is quite correct. It is true that on Bradley's theory of judgement we always predicate something of some subject. The predicate is the intentional content of the whole judgement, its subject reality. What distinguishes Bradley's theory from the traditional account is that the subject lies outside the judgement. But it is still the subject of our predication. It is important to see that in this sense Bradley would not deny that all judgement is subject–predicate in form; indeed it is precisely for this reason he thinks that it is all ultimately false. For even if, on the model of his own theory, judgements can rid themselves of their explicit subject–predicate form, they remain subject–predicate in function, and suffer from the faults of that theory. In particular, even if the content could be perfected, it would still be different from the reality it is supposed to predicate. Thus, although the traditional subject–predicate model is not his preferred theory of judgement, the faults of that theory finally catch up with us.

[19] Sprigge (1979), 152.

3.2 SUBSTANTIVE AND ADJECTIVE

3.21 *Things and their Properties*

This critique of subject–predicate grammar, however, does not exhaust all that Bradley had to say about predication. In the second chapter of *Appearance and Reality* he attacks the ontological correlate of subject–predicate grammar, the metaphysical model of a thing and its qualities, or what he calls the 'substantive and adjective' schema.

The connection between this attack and that on the grammar is easy to see. For, as we have argued (in Chapter 1) his logical studies both lead into and are founded upon his metaphysics. That is to say, the reason why we use subject–predicate grammar is because we conceptualize reality in this way. And we take reality in this way because that is how we think. Thus the two conceptions mutually support each other. Therefore to complete his attack Bradley proceeds to criticize this ontological model of the structure of reality.

3.22 *The Arguments*

Bradley's critique of this schema proceeds by listing a series of attempts to understand it, each of which he finds unsatisfactory. This argument by enumeration might be thought to be inconclusive, in that he has simply failed to find a satisfactory answer. But the way in which he characterizes the alternatives, and the objections that he raises, are such that it is clear that he thought this argument to be general in its significance.

What does it mean to speak of a thing and its qualities? What does it mean, for instance, to say of a lump of sugar that it is sweet, white, and hard? Although we use the word 'is', we are not identifying the thing with either just one or all of these qualities. A lump of sugar is not sweetness, whiteness, and hardness. It has a unity which is more than just an enumeration of qualities, and it has a particularity which is more than just abstract properties.

In order to avoid these suggestions of identity, perhaps it would be better to say that sugar has, or possesses, these qualities. But this will not do either. For such words suggest that sugar is something separate from its properties. And, indeed, if it is not identical with them, what else can it be but separate from them? But this is not the case. It seems quite wrong to say that sugar is any thing besides its qualities. For what else is there? Take away the qualities and you take away the thing.

Perhaps there is a middle path, another way of understanding the claim that sugar is or has these properties. A thing, we might say, is a group of qualities coexisting or united in a certain way: a set of properties in relation. That is to say, a group of qualities instantiated, and related together in an instance. This sounds good. But we need to ask what it really means, and, claims Bradley, 'when we leave phrases we wander among puzzles' (*AR* 16).

If we try to tighten things up, there is one question we must ask. Is this relation something separate from the qualities or not? Let us first begin by supposing that it is not. But this does not seem to work. If we take any one quality, then it certainly does seem to be something separate from that. We say that 'A is in relation R to B', but cannot accept that 'in relation R to B is A'. This reversibility test shows us that the relation is not to be identified with any one quality. Perhaps then in saying that it is nothing separate from the qualities we mean that it is nothing separate from the set of them, so that what we are really saying in, for example, the case of an object with only two properties, A and B, is that 'A and B are in relation R'. But what does it mean to take these qualities, A and B, together? If the relation is nothing separate from the qualities, then the set A and B is just the related pair. But in that case we have explained nothing, for we have simply repeated ourselves by saying, 'A-and-B-in-relation-R are in relation R'. We are nowhere nearer an analysis of the situation.

It might be thought that, rather than saying that a quality is related, we should say that it has a relation. But what does this mean? If the relation is not identical with its subject, it must be something different. When we try to cash out metaphors, this is all we get. Let us then suppose that the relation is more or less independent of its terms. But this does not work either, for then we have not connected them at all. We have three elements—that is, two terms and a relation—but no idea of how they all stand to each other. Indeed it looks as if we are in need of some new relations to connect the original relation to its terms, yet this would be to launch ourselves upon a regress. This is Bradley's infamous 'chain argument', which will be discussed in more detail in the next chapter.

The situation can be summed up like this. Predication falls foul of what Bradley calls 'the old dilemma', that is to say, 'If you predicate what is different, you ascribe to the subject what it is *not*; and if you predicate what is *not* different, you say nothing at all' (*AR* 17). Relations looked to be a solution, but on closer inspection they just postponed the problem. They simply pretend to be a solution by refusing to address the old dilemma. However, they must be brought before it. 'The thing with its adjectives is a device for enjoying at once both variety and concord' (*AR* 19–20), says Bradley. But he continues, 'The whole device is a clear makeshift. It consists in saying to the outside world, "I am the owner of these my adjectives", and to the properties, "I am but a relation, which leaves you at liberty". And to itself and for itself it is the futile pretence to have both characters at once' (*AR* 19). The qualities try both to adhere to each other and to be separate from each other. Neither of these things on its own suffices, but they cannot be combined. Thus, he claims, we are forced to see that the idea of 'a relation standing alongside of its terms is a delusion' (*AR* 18).

3.23   A Common Objection

At this point we may usefully consider another objection, also originating from Russell, that is commonly raised against Bradley. Bradley has often been accused in this argument of confusing predication and identity. Indeed, if we look at the 'old dilemma', it seems only to be a dilemma on this confusion. Russell certainly believed that this was Bradley's mistake, as it had been Hegel's before him.[20]

But, if we consider this charge in the abstract, it seems quite incredible. The whole force of the argument in chapter II of *Appearance and Reality* has been to the effect that identity will not do as analysis of predication. (He uses the reversibility test to

---

[20] Russell (1956*a*), 245. Many others have thought the 'old dilemma' confuses predication and identity, including Pringle Pattison (1902), 111; Swabey (1919), 407; Ewing (1934), 150; Church (1942*a*), 17–18; (1942*b*), 28; Walsh (1964), 433; Wollheim (1969), 71; Airaksinen (1975), 18; Martin (1977), 298; Blanshard (1984), 217–18.

determine the difference between predication and identity (*AR* 17).) Moreover, if we look back to the attack on subject–predicate grammar, we find (in two separate locations (*PL* 22–6, 370–88)) a clear rejection of the identity analysis of predication. To complete the case, if we go back one further step to his logic, we find an unequivocal rejection of the very idea of abstract identity (*PL* 141).

Yet, despite this clear evidence to the contrary, the belief that he confuses these two senses of 'is' has been so prevalent that we have to ask why this should have been so widely believed. The explanation is partly external—the influence of Russell—but it is also internal—some of the things Bradley says could be taken at least on the surface to suggest such a confusion.

He clearly accepts that in all judgement there must be an identity. 'An identity must underlie every judgement' (*PL* 28); 'Without the statement or implication of identity no judgement can be made' (*PL* 373); 'it is idle from the outside to say to thought, "Well, unite but do not identify"' (*AR* 505). But to over-concentrate on this demand distorts the wider picture. Judgement is not just an identity, for that is impossible: 'It is identical, not because it is simply the same, but because it is the same amid diversity' (*PL* 28). Were there, in thought, a similar tendency to try to do without diversity, Bradley would have insisted just as strongly that all judgements must assert diversity.

The belief that he confused identity and predication is also fuelled by terminological confusion. This may be seen by considering the 'old dilemma' itself. It should be clear that this is merely a repetition of the prohibition on abstract identity and difference that we discussed in Chapter 2. A = A says nothing, while A = B is a contradiction. But that does not depend upon their terms being linked by an identity sign. This may seem to be the case. But, if we concentrate on the earlier argument, and especially the reasons for the prohibition, we see that this is not in fact so. A = A is ruled out because it says nothing; because it requires no movement of thought. But this is not peculiar to its being an identity statement; there are many other kinds of statement which might be thought to be equally vacuous, for instance (in the notion of modern propositional logic[21]), A and A, if A then A, A if and only if A.

---

[21] In general, it should be noted that Bradley's handling of symbols is not very rigorous. This is one of the greatest differences between his own and Russell's styles of doing philosophy.

All of these are equally empty and to be excluded. In saying that he excludes identities, Bradley means any attempt to combine identical items in a single judgement, not just judgements that explicitly identify them. A similar situation occurs with contradiction. If there is nothing in common with A and B, then B is equivalent to not-A. This rules out A = B, but, as Bradley notes, it just as much rules out A and B. It would also exclude any other attempt to bring these differences together in a single judgement.

Both identity and difference must somehow be combined together in judgement. But, despite a very great emphasis on identity and difference, Bradley does not believe that this is what all judgements assert; it is rather something that they imply. Even when they assert one, the other is presupposed:

Where sameness is asserted difference is presupposed. Where difference is asserted there is a basis of sameness which underlies it. And it follows as a consequence that, if you do not mind your implications being put on a level with your meanings, you can show every judgement in the form of difference united by identity (*PL* 373).

3.3 A PUZZLE EXPLAINED

Predication, then, is claimed to be impossible, both as a system of judgement and as an ontology, because it attempts to combine identity and difference. This might seem puzzling. Did we not say in the last chapter that this was precisely the nature of reality, that identity and difference imply one another? So, in trying to combine these, is thought thus not missing, but precisely hitting, its mark?

In order to dissolve this puzzle we need to bring in once again the distinction between thought and reality. Reality is indeed an identity in diversity, so this is the goal of thought. None the less, it is, for thought, an unobtainable goal. This is because ideas (the vehicles of thought) are by nature divisive. They divide themselves both one from another and from reality. Each is itself and not another and not its object. Thus, for thought, identity and difference *are* opposed; that is to say, thought uses abstract identity and difference. Thought recognizes no middle ground between the two. Of course, ultimately they are two sides of the same coin, and thought in opposing them falsifies reality. But, from the point of view of thought, predication, in attempting to combine them, is trying to do something impossible.

Identity-in-difference is felt, but it cannot be thought. 'That on which my view rests is the immediate unity which comes in feeling . . . and the word "idea" means that the original unity has so far been broken,' says Bradley. Though it aims to do so, thought cannot repair the damage: 'aiming to reconstitute with its ideas the concrete whole of one and many, it fails, and it sinks through default into the abstract identity of predicate with subject. But this is a result at which it did not aim and cannot accept as true' (*ETR* 230–2). Thus thought is forced to use abstract identity.

Not only is thought forced to accept identities which are not also differences; it is forced to accept differences which are not also identities. That is, it is also forced to use abstract difference. Of course, many differences are overcome, and shown not to be opposed. But some, such as the differences between thought and reality itself, cannot be reconciled because they are necessary products of thinking itself, and thus, says Bradley, always some 'connections in the end must remain in part mere syntheses . . . nowhere satisfied in full' (*AR* 507–8).

Hence he concludes, 'The real is inaccessible by way of ideas' (*PL* 63). The intellect remains subject to inescapable contradictions, but, since the demand to overcome contradiction is paramount, this can only be achieved in a realm beyond thought, so thought must be transcended. Thus we find, in Bradley's philosophy, two worlds, one of identity-in-difference and one of abstract identity: the world of reality and the world of thought. This allows us to clear up one further puzzle. In the literature we find the conflicting claims both that Bradley's system of philosophy is based on abstract identity and that it is based on identity-in-difference.[22] Both are true, but at different levels. Thought operates with abstract identity. But ultimate reality uses identity-in-difference. This is what thought aims at and what convicts it. But it only fails, setting the whole process off, because it uses abstract identity and difference. It will be noted that we find exactly the same situation in the argument against relations, where he both rejects and finds himself impaled upon the distinction between internal and external relations.

---

[22] Contrast Pringle Pattison ((1902), 110–14) and Church (1942*b*).

In this chapter we have seen how Bradley attacks the subject–predicate model of understanding. During the course of this attack Bradley concludes that his puzzles about predication are better seen as a species of the more general problem about relations. It is to this problem that we turn in the next chapter.

4
Terms and Relations

THE pluralist world-view involves not just a multiplicity of separately existing subjects, individuated by their differing properties or arrangements of properties, but also a system of relations between them. They may be bigger or wiser than one another, they may be next to or after one another, they may cause or love one another, or stand to one another in any one of an infinity of other possible relations. Bradley was a no less savage critic of this picture than of its subject–predicate partner. His arguments against relations captured the attention of philosophers for many years, and are still today the most widely known part of his work.

Whatever its level of acceptance among his own philosophical generation, Bradley's whole doctrine of relations was severely criticized by that which followed. Since it was this generation that won the day, turning philosophy in a new direction, which assumed at its very basis the reality and coherence of relations, the net result was that few philosophers today consider the question of relations to be either very important or difficult. But, before we dismiss it, we should recall that his earliest critics, though far from agreeing with him, did not take this attitude. They never doubted that Bradley's challenge was both serious and difficult. For instance, Russell wrote, as late as 1924:

The subject of relations is difficult, and I am far from claiming to be now clear about it. . . . The question of relations is one of the most important that arise in philosophy, as most other issues turn on it; monism and pluralism; the question whether anything is wholly true except the whole of truth, or wholly real except the whole of reality; idealism and realism, in some of their forms; perhaps the very existence of philosophy as a subject distinct from science and possessing a method of its own.[1]

On the surface of things, Bradley's treatment of relations might appear to be divided into two apparently unconnected parts. First, there is a discussion of the subject in *Appearance and Reality*

[1] Russell (1956*b*), 333.

aimed to prove the unreality of relations. Secondly, there is a series of discussions centring around the issue of internal and external relations. We shall discuss these two parts in turn, and then examine the connections between them.

4.1 QUALITIES AND RELATIONS

In the third chapter of *Appearance and Reality*, having discussed predication, Bradley goes on to consider the topic of relations. This ordering is not accidental, for, as we saw in the last chapter, subject–predicate thought evolves into relational thought. But it does not thereby escape contradiction. On the contrary, it runs straight into the arms of its ultimate condemnation. Bradley now turns to consider this condemnation in greater detail.

This is why the third chapter covers some of the same ground as the second, as some of the earlier arguments are generalized and strengthened. It is also why in this third chapter he speaks of relations and qualities, rather than, as might be expected, relations and terms. Yet the chapter is not mere repetition, for Bradley now has a larger target in view, of which the relation of subject to predicate is but one instance. He now wants to show that a complex of elements in relation is not only incapable of being the true explanation of the existence of a thing and its properties, but that it is incapable of being a true explanation of anything whatsoever. Thus, with Bradley's discussion of relations, we reach the very heart of his metaphysics.

Bradley's argument in *Appearance and Reality* has the following structure. He claims that, taken either together or separately, qualities and relations are impossible, and that this fact may be seen, as he puts it, both from the side of qualities and from that of relations. This gives us a sequence of four arguments: qualities without relations are impossible, qualities with relations are impossible, relations without qualities are impossible, relations with qualities are impossible. 'Such rigorous schematization does not arouse confidence,' says Wollheim. 'One cannot avoid the suspicion that something in the way of accuracy of argument must have been sacrificed to preserve the architectonic quality of the whole.'[2]

---

[2] Wollheim (1969), 109.

Such a suspicion would be justified were this a case of schematization for its own sake, but, as we shall show below,[3] that is not
in fact the case. Thus, for the moment, and in hope of future
explanation, let us simply follow the arguments in the order they
appear. Such an exercise is well worth undertaking, for they have
received an undeservedly bad press over the years, and on closer
examination they turn out to be surprisingly subtle and resistant
to any swift and high-handed dismissal.

4.11 *Qualities without Relations*

First of all, claims Bradley, 'to find qualities without relations is
surely impossible' (*AR* 22). In this he seems to be quite correct; we
never do come across unrelated qualities, for wherever there is
a plurality of qualities there exist at least relations of identity and
difference, or similarity and likeness, if not any of the many other
possible relations, among them. As a matter of fact this seems
undeniable.

It might be objected that the fact that we never find them so
does not mean that they could not exist, for are we not capable
of abstracting the one from the other in thought and considering
it in isolation? Can we not consider one thing as it is in itself
regardless of how it may stand to other things? Bradley responds
to this objection by saying that we cannot separate the product,
from the process, of abstraction. That is to say, the abstracted idea
is not given to us, but exists only through and in so far as it is
maintained by the process of abstraction. But this is to say that
it exists only in relation to the process of abstraction. Hence he
argues that not only do we not experience qualities in the absence
of relations, but also that we cannot conceive them thus.

There are two further points that need to be made about this
argument. First, it has been objected that, for all his strictures on
abstraction, Bradley has not demonstrated any logical contradiction in the idea that the universe might contain but a single term
without any relations.[4] But, if there could exist one term in the
absence of all relations, why not more?

It is quite true that Bradley does not exclude the possibility of
a single term unrelated to anything else, but there is no reason

---

[3] See §4.25.   [4] Kulkarni (1957), 102.

why he should wish to do that. The fact that the world is quali-
tatively diverse, rather than an undifferentiated or homogeneous
whole, is for Bradley, something given to us by our actual experience, not logic. And, furthermore, the fact that any one term could
exist without relations in no way implies that two or more could
do so at the same time. This is because the inability of qualities
to exist without relations is a function, not of the nature of qualities,
but of the nature of plurality. What holds of them singly does not
necessarily hold of them in the plural, for, he says, 'Their plurality
gets for us all its meaning through relations' (*AR* 22).

The second point to note is that in putting forward this argument Bradley has to be careful here, for he himself later wants to
admit the existence of non-relational diversities, both within immediate experience and within the Absolute. He attempts to keep
this avenue open by distinguishing between the notion of different
qualities and that of differences. Immediate experience and the
Absolute are non-relational states, but this, he argues, does not
prevent them from containing differences, merely from containing
different qualities. The idea here is that the notions of quality and
relation belong together as two halves of an ultimately unsucces-
ful attempt to represent in thought a more basic and non-
conceptualizable difference found in immediate experience and in
the Absolute. They emerge together out of the former and evolve
together into the latter. Going below or above the realm of relations consequently takes us beyond the realm of distinguishable
qualities as well (for these are two sides of a single coin), but it
does not take us beyond difference itself. It is a fair suspicion that
this distinction between different qualities and differences is a simply verbal one, but a suspicion that can only be addressed in the
context of the wider picture.

4.12   *Qualities with Relations*

Bradley's second argument aims to show that the coexistence of
qualities with relations is impossible, this time from the side of
qualities. He argues as follows:

The qualities must be, and must *also* be related. But there is hence a
diversity which falls inside each quality. Each has a double character, as
both supporting and as being made by the relation . . . If we call its diverse aspects *a* and α, then *A* is partly each of these . . . *A* is really both

somehow together as *A* (*a* − α) . . . *without* the use of a relation it is impossible to predicate this variety of *A*. And, on the other hand, *with* an internal relation *A*'s unity disappears, and its contents are dissipated in an endless process of distinction. *A* at first becomes *a* in relation with α, but these terms themselves fall hopelessly asunder. We have got, against our will, not a mere aspect, but a new quality *a*, which itself stands in relation; and hence (as we saw before with *A*) its content must be manifold . . . We, in brief, are led by a principle of fission which conducts us to no end. (*AR* 26)

In other words, as a term standing in some relation, *A* must have two aspects, *a* and α. But, since these two aspects must be somehow related together within *A*, they themselves will of necessity each have two aspects. These in turn must be related together, launching us on an unending process of division and subdivision.

It is clear that the acceptability of this reasoning, which we might call Bradley's 'internal diversity argument', will depend in large part upon what we understand by the two aspects which any related term is said to possess, and upon whether it is true that any related term must in this way be divided. Unfortunately, it is far from clear what Bradley means here. Let us, therefore, consider a number of possible interpretations.

A common interpretation is to take the two aspects, *a* and α, as that which in the term acts as the ground or support of the relation in question, and that which may be seen as its effect or result.[5] This fits in with the text, for he describes these aspects 'as both supporting and as being made by the relation', or as 'condition and result'. Again, he says that, 'As *a* it is the difference on which distinction is based, while as α it is the distinctness that results from connexion' (*AR* 26). The problem with this interpretation is that it seems to make the argument obviously invalid, for these aspects, although characterized as different, are clearly the same. For instance, if *A* is larger than *B*, this difference is grounded in *A*'s greater size, but this is precisely the distinction between them that we note when we differentiate *A* and *B* on the basis of this relation. That the argument thus interpreted is invalid is not, of course, enough to show that it is not Bradley's own. Nevertheless, this cannot be the right interpretation, for Bradley says that 'these different aspects are not each the other' (*AR* 26).

[5] Wollheim (1969), 114; Blanshard (1984), 216; McHenry (1992), 75.

A slightly different interpretation would be to see the difference as that between *A* as something related, and *A* as something abstracted from its relations.[6] This might be suggested by his claim that '*A* is both made, and is not made, what it is by relation' (*AR* 26). On this way of looking at the matter, the first aspect would comprise all the qualitative characteristics of *A*, which would also be found in the second aspect, but there along with *A*'s relational characteristics. That is to say, the second aspect would cover all qualities of *A*, while the first would be a non-relational abstraction from the second. This interpretation is better, in that it does not involve the argument in any immediate invalidity. But none the less it cannot be correct, for Bradley says, not only that the two aspects are distinct from each other, but also that neither on its own is *A*, 'nor again is either *A*' (*AR* 26). But that conflicts with this understanding of the second aspect.

What Bradley is thinking of is clearly two parts, separate from each other, neither on its own *A*, but together making *A*. I suggest that this is best interpreted as that part of *A* affected by the relation, and that part of *A* unaffected by the relation, or, to put it another way, that part of *A* which actively enters into the particular relational situation in question and that part which remains outside. An example may make this clearer. If *A* is shorter than one metre, the two parts would be *A*'s height and all the rest of *A*'s properties. That *A* stands in the relation of being shorter than one metre tells us about *A*'s height, but, since *A* is more than just its height, it does not tell us all about *A*. Thus *A* is both 'made' and 'not made' by its relation. But, if *A*'s height is the consequence of, or made by, this relation, since it could not *just* have this height and hence stand in this relation—the height must after all be the height of something—the rest of *A*'s properties may truly be said to ground or support this relation. Although it must be admitted that Bradley's meaning here is not overly clear, this does seem to be the best interpretation.

Thus interpreted, the argument seems to be valid, and its regress is certainly not benign, for the extra relations introduced at each stage are new ones required to explain, but not explained by, those we already have. Yet is the argument sound? The most natural place to challenge it would seem to be the assumption that

[6] Ewing (1934), 148.

every related term must break up into these two aspects, for would it not be possible to relate two wholly simple terms? But I think that this line of objection is misguided, in that the whole argument is really functioning as a *reductio ad absurdum* of this very assumption. It forms a pair with his fourth attack, which we shall call the 'chain argument'. Together they present us with a dilemma. Either the relations do not affect the internal structure of their terms, or they do. The chain argument dismisses the former alternative, while this argument dismisses the latter.

4.13　Relations without Qualities

Next, Bradley claims that there could be no relations without terms. 'A relation, we must say, without qualities is nothing'; it is 'mere verbiage' (*AR* 27). He finds this too absurd to argue against in detail, but gives sufficient hints as to what worries him about it. It is, he claims, 'a false abstraction'. We find such things in reality no more than we find qualities without relations. Moreover, just as with the case of unrelated qualities, to imagine them is to abstract from our experience and carries no implication that they could really exist anywhere except in our minds.

Most critics have seen this as a minor argument, included only for the sake of architectonic completeness, for the claim seems to be obvious—unless it is connecting some terms, what is meant by calling something a relation?—and without point—who could ever deny this? But, on closer examination, there turns out to be more to this argument than that. This came out much later when, in the *Essays on Truth and Reality*, Bradley accused Russell of making precisely this mistake. For he felt that it was a consequence of Russell's realism about relations that a relation must be conceivable without its terms, in precisely the way that he had attacked in *Appearance and Reality*. He thought, moreover, that Russell had argued for this possibility (*ETR* 291, 295). We shall examine below[7] in just what sense this might be a consequence of Russell's views, but for the moment let us consider the two arguments of Russell which Bradley identifies as in defence of this position and consequently rejects.

Russell is aiming to argue that we are acquainted with universals

---

[7] See §4.14.

and not just instances of them, and this includes relations. On the specific question of relations he argues first that 'we often know propositions in which the relation is the subject, or in which the relata are not definite given objects, but "anything"'.[8] Bradley's response to this is reminiscent of Berkeley. There is, he says, no such thing as a bare universal. Whenever we think, we think only of particulars, or, as he puts it, in whatever we think of there is always an aspect of particularity. I may ignore this, or, recognizing it, treat it as irrelevant (*ETR* 299), but, if that gives me the impression of acquaintance with bare universals, such as relations, the impression is an ultimately misleading one.

Russell's second argument is that 'we should not understand the analysis if we were not acquainted with the meaning of the terms employed', which he understands as being acquainted with the universals in question. Bradley is unpersuaded by this, because he does not accept Russell's view of analysis. For Bradley, 'every analysis proceeds from and on the basis of a unity' (*ETR* 300), so that it makes no sense to speak of acquaintance with the meaning of each term individually, in separation from its context. Thus he rejects the suggestion of bare relations without terms.

4.14 *Relations with Qualities*

Bradley's fourth argument aims to show that the coexistence of relations with qualities is impossible, this time from the side of relations. He here repeats an argument already given in Chapter 3:[9]

Let us abstain from making the relation an attribute of the related, and let us make it more or less independent. 'There is a relation *C*, in which *A* and *B* stand; and it appears with both of them.' But here again we have made no progress. The relation *C* has been admitted different from *A* and *B*, and no longer is predicated of them. Something, however, seems to be said of this relation *C*, and said, again, of *A* and *B*. And this something is not to be the ascription of one to the other. If so, it would appear to be another relation, *D*, in which *C*, on one side, and, on the other side, *A* and *B*, stand. But such a makeshift leads at once to the infinite process. The new relation *D* can be predicated in no way of *C*, or of *A* and *B*; and hence we must have recourse to a fresh relation, *E*, which comes

---

[8] Russell (1910–11), 111.   [9] See pp. 78–9.

between *D* and whatever we had before. But this must lead to another, *F*; and so on, indefinitely. (*AR* 17–8)

In other words, to relate *A* and *B* we need a relation *C*, but to relate *C* and either *A* or *B* we need a new relation *D*, and so on regressively. The picture he uses is of attempting to join the last links of two ends of a chain. We might try to unite these by a third link, but this link has two ends, both of which require links to unite them to the ends of the chain, and so on (*AR* 28). Let us, therefore, refer to this as his 'chain argument'.

This is perhaps Bradley's most notorious argument, regularly brought out as a stock example of philosophical confusion. Broad, for instance, said that 'Charity bids us avert our eyes from the pitiable spectacle of a great philosopher using an argument which would disgrace a child or a savage.'[10] I think that, on the contrary, this is one of the most powerful of Bradley's arguments, and that it has been consistently undervalued. I shall show this by defending it against objections. There have been essentially two kinds of objection to the argument.

The first kind of objection rejects the whole regress as a mistake caused by treating relations as though they were just further terms. Russell puts it this way: 'Bradley conceives a relation as something just as substantial as its terms, and not radically different in kind.'[11] It is only on this assumption that any regress occurs, he thinks. But this objection is highly confused, in two respects.

First, as we suggested above, the chain argument forms but one half of a pair of arguments (the other half being the internal diversity argument). Bradley may be represented as asking but one simple question: if we list the world's contents, do we find relations as a separate element or not? The 'chain argument' argument deals with a 'yes' answer, the 'internal diversity argument' with a 'no' answer. If the answer is 'yes', we need to know how these separate elements stand to their terms, but, if the answer is 'no', we need to understand how it is that they simultaneously characterize both the term and its context without introducing a diversity into the former. Whatever we take relations to be, this seems a legitimate question, that, on pain of self-contradiction, must be answered one way or the other. Bradley himself sees insurmountable problems with either answer, and thus to criticize this argument

[10] Broad (1933), 85.   [11] Russell (1927), 263.

for treating relations as separate elements is simply to agree with him that this side of the dilemma is a dead end.

The second confusion might be put like this. Simply to answer 'yes' to Bradley's question is not *in itself* to commit some philosophical blunder of the kind Russell is speaking, for he *himself* thought that relations were independent entities. He thinks that he has avoided Bradley's argument because he imagines relations to be 'radically different in kind'. But what he fails to see is that this aspect of his conception is irrelevant, for Bradley's argument applies against *any* account which takes relations to be separate elements of reality, be they 'as substantial as their terms' *or* 'radically different in kind'.

The second kind of objection to this argument is more subtle. It accepts that there is indeed a regress, but counters that it is a benign regress of verbal implications not a vicious one of ontological presuppositions. How is R related to A and B? We can, if we want to, say that there is another relation here, but there is no real need to say this—it is simply a verbal move. The series of 'new' intermediate relations do not add anything not present in the original relation. Just as not-not-A, not-not-not-not-A, not-not-not-not-not-A, etc., differ in merely verbal form from A; $AR'RR'B$, $AR''R'R''RR''R'R''B$, etc., are all equivalent in sense to ARB, differing merely in their form of expression. This is the essence of Cook Wilson's objection.[12]

Yet this objection also fails to see that the argument here is addressed to one side of a particular dilemma. This line of objection has not yet been pushed as far as it can go. If the addition of R', R'', R''', etc., adds nothing not already present in their terms, then how can the addition of R, the first of this regressive series of relations? The situation is perhaps analogous to that with the predicate 'is true'. ' "P is true" is true' says no more than 'P is true', and for the very same reason it also says no more than 'P'. But, if the inclusion of R is a merely verbal step, then what in effect we are saying is that no analysis of a relational situation need include anything more than its terms. This, however, is something that is argued against in the 'internal diversity argument'. If, on the other hand, R does add something not already present in its terms, so that it is a real, rather than a merely verbal, addition, then what

---

[12] Cook Wilson (1926), ii. 692–5. See also Wollheim (1969), 114.

reason can there be for not continuing with the regress, and saying the same of R', R'', R''', etc.? In short we might say: either we refuse to get on board at all, or we go to the end of the line; what we cannot do is go one stop down the line and get off. That is the dilemma.

4.15   *The Unreality of Relations*

From these four arguments Bradley draws the following uncompromising lesson. 'The conclusion to which I am brought is that a relational way of thought—any one that moves by the machinery of terms and relations—must give appearance, and not truth. It is a makeshift, a device, a mere practical compromise, most necessary, but in the end most indefensible' (*AR* 28). It is a device for combining together the irreconcilable ideas of unity and diversity—that is to say, the ideas of diverse terms and of the unified complex they somehow form when related together by a relation. We succeed in this 'merely by shutting the eye, which if left open would condemn us; or by a perpetual oscillation and a shifting of the ground, so as to turn our back upon the aspect we desire to ignore' (*AR* 28). Metaphysics forces us to face up to this contradiction, and the consequence that ultimate reality cannot be relational. Not surprisingly this denial of the reality of relations met with fierce resistance from realist quarters. Let us consider two such objections.

One objection would be that, in asking for an explanation of how relations work, Bradley is asking for the impossible. It is simply the business of relations to relate. They are, it might be said, conceptually too basic to be reduced to anything else. Bradley was aware of this response and attempted to counter it. 'It can hardly be maintained that this character calls for no understanding,' he claimed, 'for it most evidently has ceased to be something quite immediate' (*AR* 21). What he means is that relations do not form a part of the raw and uninterpretable base data of perceptual experience. Rather they are a metaphysical construct that we arrive at through reflection on that experience. This seems correct. But it is not only highly evasive to refuse to analyse relations. A second problem with this response is that it is inconsistent. In introducing relations we seem to be introducing special entities with magical connecting powers. But, if there can be magical connections between separate entities, then we can always attribute these to the terms and their predicates directly, so that we do not need relations as separate entities at all, and there is no need to go beyond the terms and their predicates. But this position is argued against in the 'internal diversity argument'. A third problem with this stance is that it misconstrues Bradley's objection to relations. His worry is not just that he does not understand how they work; rather his point is that it seems as though they cannot work, for, he thinks, they are trying to do something quite impossible.

A second kind of objection consists in simply pointing out the utter absurdity of his conclusion. Historically this was a very significant argument, for looking at the literature of the time you see that his critics had few other arguments against him. Moore and Russell triumphed over Bradley, not because of their critiques of his arguments, but because they saw that the sheer implausibility of his conclusions was an argument against them. Russell distinguishes between two kinds of philosophy, which he calls the classical and the empirical traditions. While it is characteristic of the classical school to attempt to prove matters of fact a priori, advocates of the empirical tradition, with their knowledge of the long history of a priori errors refuted by experience, find it 'natural to suspect a fallacy in any deduction of which the conclusion appears to contradict patent facts'.[13] Here we find a great gulf between Bradley and modern philosophy, for he simply would not accept this method of arguing (*AR* 485). The best, or the worst (depending on your view), but certainly the most notable, feature of Bradley's philosophy is his willingness to follow arguments to their conclusion. If a choice had to be made between a great historical fact and a high abstract principle, then, says Bradley, 'this issue I must decide in favour of the principle and of the higher truth' (*PL* 686). It is this faith in the power of abstract reasoning that leads people to classify him along with the other great a priori metaphysicians of the history of philosophy.

In his defence, however, we should not over-exaggerate the implausibility of his conclusion. In saying that relations are not real, Bradley is not denying that they appear to us, simply that they possess ultimate reality. In this sense his denial could be compared

[13] Russell (1914), 7.

with, for instance, Locke's denial that objects are coloured. Locke has no intention of denying that objects appear coloured to us (nor even that there is anything in them which explains this); he is simply claiming that nothing like phenomenal colour will appear in any ultimate account of reality. Bradley thinks the same about relations. His theory of appearance will be discussed in greater detail in Chapter 7.

4.2 INTERNAL AND EXTERNAL RELATIONS

The attack in chapter III of *Appearance and Reality* did not exhaust all that Bradley had to say about relations. He also wrote an important appendix to that work on the subject, several papers in response to Russell's criticisms, as well as a long essay on relations, unfinished at the time of his death, but subsequently published posthumously in his *Collected Essays*.

In these later treatments the discussions of relations take a different turn, whose connection with the arguments we have already looked at is not immediately obvious. The discussions centre around the notions of internal and external (or intrinsic and extrinsic) relations. Unfortunately, Bradley's later work on relations has engendered much confusion, both about the signification of these terms and what Bradley's position was regarding them. Not only is the terminology archaic and foreign to us, but even in its day it was not clearly understood. Moreover, Bradley himself is often vague and not always univocal in what he means. We shall therefore begin by asking just what Bradley meant by these terms.

4.21 *Internality and Externality*

What does the distinction between internal and external relations amount to for Bradley? Despite the weaknesses in Bradley's own presentation of the matter, by taking a continuous sample of his claims, a pattern emerges. For instance, in the *Principles of Logic* he says that to advocate externality is 'to fancy relations as an arbitrary network stuck on from the outside by destiny or chance, and making no reasonable difference to anything' (*PL* 289). In *Appearance and Reality* he asks the question, 'Are qualities and in general are terms altered necessarily by the relations into which they enter? In other words are there any relations which are merely extrinsical?' (*AR* 513–14). Again in the *Essays on Truth and Reality* he says that to admit externality 'is to assume that a thing's relations, which make all the difference to other things, or at least all the difference beyond itself, make no difference whatever to itself' (*ETR* 43). In the *Collected Essays* he says that, if terms are related together externally, this means 'that their coming or being together in fact, and as somehow actually in one, is due in no way to the particular characters of either the relations or the terms. From neither side will there be anything like a contribution to, or an entrance into, the other side' (*CE* 642). By contrast an internal relation is said to be one which 'essentially penetrates the being of its terms' (*AR* 347).

Putting these together, a consistent usage emerges, which may perhaps be best illustrated through an example. Let us suppose that Sally-Ann is shorter than one metre. If we now consider the possible situation in which this relation has been removed, that is to say where she is now no longer shorter than one metre, the change must make a difference to her, in particular to her height. The relation, we might say, in this sense, affects her, and is thus internal. This is to be contrasted with the case where Sally-Ann is in the kitchen. In this case removing the relation, so that she was no longer in the kitchen, would leave her unaffected. So this relation is external. On this understanding we might then say that a relation is internal if it affects its terms and external if it leaves them unaffected, or, more precisely, that a relational property P had by some particular A is internal if A would have been different had it not had P, or, what is equivalent, if anything which did not have P could not be A.[14] It is to be noted that this definition only applies to particulars, since it makes no sense to speak of altering universal or abstract objects.[15] This understanding of the distinction is certainly how many others took the terms, whether they were champions or critics of the internality of relations.[16]

At the outset this definition of what it is for a relation to be internal needs to be distinguished from two superficially similar

---

[14] Moore (1922*b*), 283.

[15] Ibid. 281; Ewing (1934), 131. Manser ((1983), 121–3) has argued that restriction to particulars is borne out in Bradley's use of the terms.

[16] Joachim (1906), 11; Bosanquet (1911), ii. 277; Ayer (1935).

but quite different accounts, from which it follows trivially that all relations are internal.

The first confusion is to think that, if A has a relational property P, then it must be different in at least one respect from what it would be were it not to have this relation, in precisely the fact that it does stand in this relation. This is of course true, but the difference in question is a merely trivial one. It simply shows us that we must restate the thesis as saying that the absence of the relation makes a difference *other* than simply that of not having the corresponding relational property.

The second confusion was first noted in 1919 by G. E. Moore[17] and is rather more subtle, although equally fallacious. A relational property P had by some subject A is internal if A would have been different had it not had P, or, what is equivalent, if anything which did not have P would not have been A. But there is a possible confusion which would make this obviously true, says Moore. The confusion is between the following two propositions. (1) Necessarily, if A has P, then anything which has not is other than A. This is trivially true and must be distinguished from the superficially similar proposition, (2) If A has P then anything which has not is necessarily other than A. This makes P into an internal relation and is far from obviously true. It would only be necessary that something lacking P was other than A if P were a necessary property of A. Otherwise the object could be identical with A, in those cases where A lacks P. This second thesis is quite different from the tautology that, if A has P, it cannot be identical with something that does not. Moore gives us an example. Any person who was not the father of George V must have been other than Edward VII, but, although Edward VII was in fact the father of George V, he might have existed without being the father of George V. Since (1) does not imply (2), we should not be seduced into accepting the substantial thesis because of the evident truth of the trivial thesis. Whether anyone ever actually made this confusion is less clear.

Do we now have an accurate picture of what Bradley meant by internal and external relations? I think that we do, but one objection to our way of understanding the distinction has been raised by Sprigge.[18] He claims that, in the idea of a relation that affects

[17] Moore (1922*b*) 283.
[18] Sprigge (1979). See also Sprigge (1983), ch. 5.

its terms, Bradley runs together two distinct senses in which relations may be internal, which ought to be kept separate. There are ideal relations: the relation between two items is ideal if it is explained by the character of the terms themselves. There are holistic relations: the relation between two items is holistic if their being in this relation is a matter of their being mere abstractions from a more genuine individual which embraces them both. Sprigge's purpose in making this distinction is to claim that both the legitimacy and the consequences of claiming that all relations are internal vary considerably upon which interpretation we take.[19]

As is so often the case, light may be shed on this by turning to the *Principles of Logic*. Manser[20] has shown how the definition of relations as holistic can be traced back into Bradley's logical investigations. The terms internal and external do not figure heavily in the early work. Nevertheless, Manser has argued that the origins of the distinction can indeed be found there. He claims that the demand for internal relations began life as a logical thesis. As such, the point Bradley is trying to make is that all individual ideas (including those of relations) are artificial abstractions from the single idea that is involved in judgement.

However, this does not vindicate the holistic over the ideal interpretation, for Manser fails to see that the definition of internal relations as ideal can also be traced back to the early theory of judgement. Thinking about judgement, you can start from the whole and work down to the elements abstracted from it, but you can also start from the elements and work up to the whole that they imply. These are merely two sides of the same coin. But, starting from the bottom we see that, since terms cannot be joined which have nothing in common—that is contradiction—there must be a point of identity between them, which grounds their interrelation. But this is to say that the essence of a relation between some terms is to be found in the nature of the terms themselves: precisely the interpretation of relations as ideal.

Working back to their origins in the *Principles of Logic* allows us to see that these two ways of defining internal relations are not

---

[19] In particular Sprigge sees the thesis that all relations are ideal as grounded in an illegitimate use of the principle of sufficient reason. But this does not impede the monistic conclusion he wishes to draw, for that he sees as the proper consequence only of the thesis that all relations are holistic, which can, he thinks, be given a legitimate grounding in intuition.

[20] Manser (1983), ch. 7.

contrary, but rather complementary, aspects of the theory of judgement. Terms are only related because they are abstractions from the whole judgement, but it is only because the terms imply their union with each other that the judgement is a whole. And when we move from logic to metaphysics the same point still holds. These are not conflicting definitions, as Sprigge thinks, but complementary aspects of internality. If the terms are abstractions from the whole or Absolute, then they must imply or ground each other from their own natures. While at different times Bradley may emphasize one side of this relationship or another, essentially they both require each other, and neither side is ultimately more important than the other.

The transition of the distinction between internal and external relations from a logical to a metaphysical dichotomy has been characterized by Manser as a regrettable step Bradley would have done better to avoid.[21] But, given Bradley's view of the relation between thought and reality, this transition was inevitable. As we have already seen, logic aims in the end at an isomorphism, if not a fundamental identity, with metaphysics. It need not be denied that in becoming a dichotomy of characteristics within metaphysics the distinction becomes less clear. However, this lack of clarity is not as serious as it might otherwise be, for, as we shall attempt to show below,[22] a degree of vagueness can be tolerated because of the precise use to which Bradley wishes to put this distinction.

The debate about internal and external relations has suffered from much confusion. So we may close this discussion of the meaning of these terms by dismissing two wholly false, but historically quite influential, interpretations of the distinction.

First, propositions describing internal relations between terms are not simply those that can be reduced to subject–predicate ones. In his 1924 paper *Logical Atomism* Russell said that he meant by the doctrine of external relations,

Primarily this, that a relational proposition is not, in general, logically equivalent formally to one or more subject–predicate propositions. Stated more precisely: Given a relational propositional function 'x R y', it is not in general the case that we can find predicates α, β, γ, such that, for all values of x and y, x R y is equivalent to $x\alpha$, $y\beta$, $(x,y)\gamma$ (where (x,y) stands for the whole consisting of x and y), or to any one or two of these. This,

---

[21] Ibid. 131–4.　　[22] See §4.25.

and this only, is what I mean to affirm when I assert the doctrine of external relations; and this, clearly, is at least part of what Mr Bradley denies when he asserts the doctrine of internal relations.[23]

But not even this modest attribution to Bradley can be accepted. For it is clear, as we have already seen, that Bradley rejects subject–predicate propositions, and thus *a fortiori* any attempt to reduce relational ones to them. However, we can see why Russell should have made this mistake. He thinks that, because an internal relation is not an independent item, it must be a predicate of the term or pair of terms it relates. Bradley does indeed think that it is not independent, even that it is in some sense 'in' the term or pair, but he rejects the idea that it is a nameable part or predicate of the terms, taken either singly or together.

Equally mistaken is the view that simply reduces propositions describing internal relations between terms to analytic or a priori propositions. Though he is by no means the only culprit, this may be found, for instance, in Pears. He says, 'A relation is internal if the proposition attributing it to the individual is true *a priori*.'[24] As an account of actual historical usage, this is fallacious.

Bradley has in mind something different from mere analyticity. First, to claim that a relation is internal to some term is not to say that it figures explicitly as part of that term's *definition*, but rather that it belongs to the object itself. Secondly, even where this is the case, it is not to be thought of as contained in the manner of some nameable part or property. But again we can see how the error arises, especially for someone who believes that all necessity is analytic, for the distinction between a term's internal and external relations coincides with that between its essential and its accidental relational properties. Having now seen what is meant by the terms, internal and external, let us turn to consider what were Bradley's views about them.

4.22   *Objections to External Relations*

Bradley whole-heartedly opposes the idea that there might be any purely external relations, and this has become one of his best-known views. However, it should also be noted that he did not deny that there could be occasions in which speaking of external

---

[23] Russell (1956*b*), 335.   [24] Pears (1967), 162.

relations might have a clear, if limited, use (*CE* 645). But he certainly thought that, in the end, they were impossible. 'I do not admit that any relation whatever can be merely external and make no difference to its terms' (*AR* 513; cf. *PL* 290, 612; *AR* 125, 514; *ETR* 240; *CE* 643).

Why does he say this? It is often thought that this relies on some kind of appeal to the principle of sufficient reason, and certainly some of the things that he says suggest this. In a purely external relation, he objects, the terms 'seem related for no reason at all, and, so far as they are concerned, the relation seems arbitrarily made' (*AR* 514). Again he says, 'such irrationality and externality cannot be the last truth about things. Somewhere there must be a reason why this and that appear together' (*AR* 517). This may perhaps be a version of sufficient reason, but the real force behind his criticism lies, I would contend, in his understanding of contradiction, which is in turn a function of his view of negation.[25] External relations are meaningless because they attempt to combine diversity without a point of union. 'The intellect has in its nature no principle of mere togetherness . . . if in this unity no internal connexion of diversity natural to the intellect can be found, we are left with a diversity belonging to and conjoined in one undistinguished point. And this is contradiction' (*AR* 511).

The denial of external relations has been so often, and so vehemently, rejected by Bradley's critics that it has come to be believed that there exist *arguments* against it. But in fact there are none. The only objection in the literature consists in pointing to the many common-sense examples of apparently external relations. For instance, spatial relations, temporal relations, resemblances, or differences—none of these seem to affect the terms which stand in them.

However, these alleged counter-examples are no worry at all to Bradley. He considers two of them, spatial relations and resemblance, in the Appendix to *Appearance and Reality*. It might seem as though there could occur changes in the spatial or resemblance relations in which an object stood without this causing any fundamental change in the object itself. For instance, an object A seems not necessarily to undergo any non-trivial change of character in ceasing to be, for example, to the left of or the same

[25] See §§2.21, 2.23.

colour as some other object B. Bradley objects that, in such cases, while something may indeed remain the same, this is not the object itself, but a mere abstraction from it, or, as he puts it, a 'character' (*AR* 514). In other words, he sees the apparent counter-examples as just that, apparent. 'What is proved is that a certain character may, as such and in respect of that character, exist indifferently in various relations. But what is not proved at all is that this character could exist independent and naked' (*AR* 513). At no time does he deny that everyday experience presents us with external relations, only that they should be taken really to have this nature, for everyday experience deals with a world of abstractions.

For a thing may remain unaltered if you identify it with a certain character, while taken otherwise the thing is suffering change. If, that is, you take a billiard-ball and a man in abstraction from place, they will of course—so far as this is maintained—be indifferent to changes of place. But on the other hand neither of them, if regarded so, is a thing which actually exists; each is a more or less valid abstraction. But take them as existing things and take them without mutilation, and you must regard them as determined by their places and qualified by the whole material system into which they enter. (*AR* 517)

In this way, then, we see that Bradley provides himself with a mechanism to dismiss all common-sense examples of apparently external relations out of court. While at the everyday level they may concern important and useful practical or relative truths, in the last analysis they all involve abstractions, and hence cannot represent the final truth about matters.

4.23 Objections to Internal Relations

It is a common belief that Bradley held a theory of internal relations, that is to say, that he thought all relations were internal. It may therefore come as a surprise to many to find that he is an equally vehement critic of internal relations. 'Mere internal relations, then, like relations that are merely external, are untenable if they make a claim to ultimate and absolute truth' (*CE* 645; cf. *ETR* 239, 290–1).

What was his objection to internal relations? The problem, as Bradley sees it, is that the demand for internality is self-destructive to the very concept of a relation, for an internal relation must be grounded in and spring from its terms, but, if it becomes so bound up with them that it is indistinguishable from their other predicates, it becomes lost as a separately functioning element, and all you have is two terms. But without a relation there is no connection between these. In this way the notion of an 'internal relation' is at odds with itself, for the more *internal* we make it, the less of a *relation* it becomes. By analogy, it might be said that the notion of 'fair and accurate criticism' suffers from a similar kind of internal tension. To present a really fair and accurate criticism of some philosopher's views, you need to be able to see things through their eyes. This is something every critic strives towards. But in a sense the task is self-defeating. If we ever really did see through their eyes, their views would be ours, and there could be no *criticism* at all. Returning to relations, Bradley puts the matter like this:

An actual relation, we may remind ourselves, must possess at once both the characters of a 'together' and a 'between', and, failing either of these, is a relation no longer. Hence our terms cannot make a relation by passing themselves over into it bodily. For in that event their individuality, and with it the required 'between' would be lost. (CE 644)

Thus paradoxically it turns out that internal relations are impossible for precisely the same reason as external relations: 'viewed as real, each in and by itself, there is no way in which they could pass or be carried beyond themselves so as to generate a relation' (*CE* 644). External relations are unable to make any real connection with either of their terms; internal relations make a bond with their terms, but in doing so, make them unable to reach out to each other.

Bradley clearly attempted to dispel the view that he had a theory of internal relations. 'Criticism', he said, 'which assumes me committed to the ultimate truth of internal relations, all or any of them, is based on a mistake' (*ETR* 239). 'The idea, I would add, that I myself accept any such doctrine as the above seems to myself even ludicrous' (*CE* 642). It is, therefore, worth asking why this has been so widely believed about him. A full answer to this question would be extremely complicated, for there are a number of reasons. The denial of external relations, many clear demands for internality (*PL* 127; *AR* 322, 517), Joachim's and other idealists' belief in this thesis, and the interpretation of Russell and many subsequent critics have all played their part. A curious claim in the index to *Appearance and Reality* to the effect that all relations are internal can hardly have helped, but should not have been taken seriously, for Bradley prefaces that index with the following note: 'The reader who finds this collection of references useless, as well as faulty and incomplete, is requested to treat it as non-existent' (*AR* 565). But, however it may have been arrived at, this is one the commonest of all the misconceptions about Bradley's philosophy.

The truth of the matter is that, as with external relations, although Bradley thought that they could be used to convey important and useful practical or relative truths, because they involve abstractions, internal relations are incapable of representing the ultimate truth about reality.

4.24   The Impossibility of Relations

Thus, 'To take reality as a relational scheme, no matter whether the relations are "external" or "internal", seems therefore impossible and perhaps even ridiculous' (*ETR* 190). Relations cannot be exclusively one or the other, but must be both. 'No relation is *merely* intrinsic or external, and every relation is both' (*CE* 667). However, the either–or between them is unavoidable, because they undermine each other—the external is essentially not internal, and vice versa. Hence Bradley thinks that relations are contradictory and impossible. With this result we also see that, contrary to initial appearances and popular interpretation, there is no conflict between the two arguments of his earlier and later work on relations; both argue for the same conclusion: that relations, although indubitably apparent, are ultimately unreal.

As with the parallel result that we arrived at in the case of subject–predicate thought, there is an important point about levels to be made here.[26] It might seem that, in attempting to combine internal and external relations, thought is precisely succeeding, rather than failing, to capture the nature of ultimate reality, and indeed Bradley says that 'The whole "Either–or" between external and internal relations, to me seems unsound' (*ETR* 238). The point to note is that this is only so at the level of reality. Because it operates with a principle of abstract identity rather than identity-

---

[26] See §3.3.

in-difference, thought inevitably finds these two to be in opposition, and thus all relational thought stands condemned. The union of the internal and the external, like that of the one and the many, is something which can never be thought, only felt.

One final point that should be noted about Bradley's account is that he concerns himself solely with two-place relations. This is no accident, for he rejects the very possibility of a more-than-two-place relation (*ETR* 303, 306; *CE* 649, 650). He thinks that cases of apparently more than two-place relations are really complex relational situations resolvable into a number of two-place relations between either terms or other relations. Thus 'between' is not a relation connecting three terms (A is between B and C), but a complex where A is in relation to B, B is in relation to C, and the two relations are in relation to each other.

This aspect of Bradley's theory has received little attention, perhaps because the arguments that he gives for his view (*ETR* 303–9; *CE* 674) are exceedingly hard to make sense of. It may seem strange to find him, at this point, endorsing rather than opposing the analysis of complex situations into their parts, but the explanation of this seems to be that he does not regard them as any genuine advance in the direction of unity or cohesion. They can bring no more 'glue' to a set of distinct terms and two-place relations than a single dyadic relation can bring to a pair of terms, but in that case the higher level of unity that they seem to display is a sham, as hollow as the suggestion that to do the morning register at school is less work than asking each child in turn if he or she is present.

4.25 *Relation to the Debate in* Appearance and Reality

Not only does Bradley's later way of discussing relations, in terms of internality and externality, lead to the same goal as his earlier approach, but it also helps us to understand the earlier way of putting his objections, and thus arrive at the heart of the problem.

The first thing we need to see is how internality and externality may be viewed as notions of degree. It is true that there is no halfway point between belonging to a term and not belonging to it, but the fact that terms can be complex, and that relations may implicate a greater or lesser number of their constituent qualities, allows us to introduce a degree of latitude into the matter, and a sense in which relations may be more or less internal or external.

This allows us to demarcate, on paper at least, four different positions, from the fully external to the fully internal. First, a relation might be fully external, so that a relational situation involves three independent items, and the relation does not affect the terms at all. Bradley argues that in reality this is impossible, because there would be just three unconnected elements, each capable of independent existence, but, as we have seen, neither relations nor terms are capable of such independent existence. He claims that, in order to make sense of the situation, we must see the terms and relations as more closely connected than this.

Next, a relation might be partially external. In this case a measure of independence is sacrificed. The relation affects its term, but only its accidental properties and not its essence. For instance, if Sally-Ann is to the left of the dog, removing this relation, although it makes no real difference to her, does alter the list of things true of her. Bradley accepts that this way of viewing things is useful, but thinks it arbitrary. The object that it considers to be affected is not the real object—its essence remains as unaffected as before, so that we might still ask how this essence stands to the relation. Truly to connect with the term, he thinks, we need a relation, which affects more than just its accidental properties.

Thus we move to a position where the relation does affect the essence of the term. For instance, if Sally-Ann is shorter than one metre, removing this relation affects her. But Bradley objects that this relation is still only partially internal. Removing it affects Sally-Ann, but only part of her, namely her height. The relation sets up a division within the term, and is still external and unconnected to one part of it. Yet further internality is required.

Finally we link the predicate with the whole of the term, so that it merges into every part of it. The problem now is that the relation has ceased to exist as an independent entity at all. We have just two terms. Too late we realize that, in the drive for sufficient internality to make a link, we have lost the externality required for the existence of a linking element. If every aspect of Sally-Ann is but a relation to the world she inhabits, then there is no longer any difference between Sally-Ann and her world: they do not stand in any relation to one another. Thus we are placed in a dilemma.

A term in the end . . . can stand in no relation into which it itself does not enter. But on the other side, if the relation is not to be destroyed, the term's entrance cannot . . . be entire and made bodily. It must be no more than partial and confined to what we call 'a certain respect'. But the question as to how that part of the term which enters in is related to that part which remains outside leaves us . . . with a final contradiction. (*CE* 645)

It is possible to correlate each of these four positions with one of the four arguments in *Appearance and Reality*, thus connecting together Bradley's earlier and later discussions on relations. The first corresponds to the impossibility of relations without qualities, and the significance of this attack in the earlier work is thus made clear. The point is that a belief in external or separate relations implies the possibility of their independent existence. He twice describes the theory of external relations in this way (*ETR* 238, 291). The impossibility of the second case, where we can still ask how the term as a whole stands to the relation that affects only its accidental properties, corresponds to the chain argument. The impossibility of the third case, where the term itself is broken up into a part which is affected and a part which is not, corresponds to the internal diversity argument. This also allows us to confirm our interpretation of the two aspects in the internal diversity argument, as that part of the term affected, and that part unaffected, by the relation in question. The fourth case, where the relation has wholly disappeared, corresponds to the impossibility of qualities without relations.[27]

Establishing these correlations shows us that Bradley is not merely engaging in idle schematization in the earlier attack, but going through the whole range of possibilities in a systematic fashion. Significantly, we see that it also does not matter very much where

[27] McHenry ((1992), 75) accepts that the internal diversity argument and the relations without qualities argument are directed against internal and external relations respectively, but he differs in correlating the chain argument with the attack on internal relations and the qualities without relations argument with the attack on external relations. This cannot be correct. In the first case, we have only to ask how a relation stands to its terms, thus setting up a chain, if they are conceived of as relatively independent of, or *external* to, their terms. In the second case, what is distinctive about external relations is their capacity to exist in isolation from any terms, not whether the terms possess any reciprocal capacity. Rather, the significance of imagining a world which contained only terms is that, were this possible, we would already have all the material necessary to explain relational truths, *internal* to the terms themselves.

we draw the line between internal and external relations, for, wherever we draw it, neither of them can suffice. Finally, we see that, contrary to initial appearances, not only do the two arguments in fact work together towards a common goal, that relations are unreal, but they actually trace out one and the same route to that goal, merely seen from two different perspectives.

4.3 PHILOSOPHICAL MONISM

Relations then are unreal. Where does this leave us? It is usually thought that the view this leaves us with is philosophical substance monism. (Substance monists claim there is only one thing, type monists claim there is only one kind of thing.) However, this should not be accepted without thought, for the conclusion has been interestingly challenged. Silkstone[28] has argued that Bradley's attack on relations does indeed disprove pluralism, for all apparently independent entities are shown to be relative and run into others. This, however, does not yield monism, for by the very same arguments things cannot be one without also being many. To put this another way, in attacking external relations he forces things to coagulate, but in attacking internal relations, he equally forces them to separate. Thus, claims Silkstone, Bradley's line of argument leads not so much to monism as to the view that any thinking which utilizes the categories 'one' and 'many' as exclusive of each other is failing to grasp reality.

It cannot be denied that Silkstone has made a very important point here that is all too often ignored by those who simply characterize Bradley as a monist—namely, that this final position does not exclude, but in fact requires, a genuine diversity. Bradley's Absolute is not, as Russell once described it, 'some kind of Eleatic One'.[29] Unlike the homogeneous One of Parmenides, where diversity is merely an illusory appearance, diversity for Bradley is a real and essential component of the Absolute.

None the less there are problems with Silkstone's claim, for it does not square perfectly with the text. In defence of his thesis, Silkstone argues that Bradley's apparent advocacy of monism can be explained as an overstated reaction against pluralism. But is

---

[28] Silkstone (1974).   [29] Russell (1959), 290.

this really correct? It must be confessed that not all his statements and arguments may be easily read this way. Let us consider two such examples.

First, we may consider the debate over internal and external relations. So far we have represented Bradley as arguing: relations must but cannot be internal, relations must but cannot be external. Therefore relations are impossible. This form of argument seems symmetrical between monism and pluralism. But our account is not yet complete. Although he does in fact attack both external and internal relations, there seems to be a clear preference for internal ones, not yet represented on our account. He says, 'As to what has been called the axiom of internal relations, I can only repeat that "internal relations", though truer by far than "external", are, in my opinion, not true in the end' (*ETR* 312).

This claim makes the belief that he advocated a theory of internal relations, though mistaken, more understandable. The asymmetry may be incorporated by adding a dynamic nature to the paradox. This comes from his favouring internal relations, but pushing them to such a degree that all externality is lost and the relations disappear into a supra-relational whole beyond thought. The paradox thus becomes structurally the same as one he offered against morality in the *Ethical Studies* (*ES* 234–5). Relations, like morality, make on the world a demand which sows the seeds of their own ultimate destruction. And, just as morality is transcended into a supra-moral realm, the denial of relations clearly moves us in the direction of a supra-relational goal, which is a unity.

Our second example shows that it is not enough to resist the label 'monism' to point out that reality contains diversity as well as unity. Bradley considers this situation and notes that it is ambiguous. In chapter XIII of *Appearance and Reality* he asks of reality, 'Is it one system, possessing diversity as an adjective; or is its consistency, on the other hand, an attribute of independent realities?' (*AR* 124). To play on the Hegelian phase, we might ask, is it a one-in-many or a many-in-one? Bradley considers this choice. It hinges, he thinks, on the question, is a plurality of reals possible? But this, he argues emphatically, is not possible. Such reals would have to be independent or self-sufficient. But that is not all. They would also have to coexist together. Yet there is no way of doing this without introducing relations of coexistence, which destroy their independence. It therefore looks as if there could not exist a plurality of reals (*AR* 124–6), and thus it seems as if Bradley is indeed advocating monism. Reality, although also many, is more fundamentally one. He says, 'the Real is qualified by all plurality. It owns this diversity while itself it is not plural' (*AR* 461).

If, at the end of the day, the critic persists in asking, was Bradley a monist, I cannot help thinking that this question is a rather pointless and largely verbal one. How you answer it all depends on how you define your terms, and there is no one obvious definition. If we think of substance monists as those who say that the world's things are but one in number, and pluralists as those who claim that there are many things, the whole point clearly hangs on the meaning of the word 'thing'. There are at least three ways to take this word, but no one more obviously correct than the other two.

If we take 'thing' in the Aristotelian sense of a subject of properties, or a subject of judgement, then, for Bradley, there is only one thing. In his theory, reality is the only property-bearer, and, in judgement, the entire content of any thought is predicated of one subject—reality as a whole.

If we take 'thing' as some kind of an independent existence, rather like 'substance' in the philosophy of Spinoza or Leibniz, then again he is a monist. In his system only the Absolute possesses this kind of independence. He commonly identifies 'reality' with such particularity, individualness, or self-subsistence, and it is this definition that he uses in the argument above to disprove pluralism, or what he calls a plurality of reals.

If, on the other hand, you take a 'thing' to be merely some differentiation or group of differentiations among the world's contents (perhaps certain coexistences of distinguishable qualities), then his monism becomes less obvious. He would resist any suggestion that these differentiations are lost in the whole, that the whole is homogeneous in this respect. They may in some sense become one—but, he would want to add, they also remain many.

With Bradley's attack on relations, we have completed the project begun in Chapter 2—that is to say, we have explained Bradley's view of the nature of both reality and thought and explained why he thought that they could never be identified. This provides us with the framework of his metaphysics, some further features of which we shall now explore.

5

Space and Time

BRADLEY's arguments against the reality of space and time have received little attention (in comparison with, for instance, McTaggart's attack on the reality of time). In this chapter I want to argue that they are deserving of more serious philosophical consideration. This is so in at least two respects.

First, Bradley's arguments against space and time are connected with his attack on relations. They are, he says in chapter IV of *Appearance and Reality*, merely 'a peculiar form of the problem which we discussed in the last chapter' (*AR* 31)—that is, the problem of terms and relations. But he is not simply arguing (as he could have done): space and time involve relations, relations are unreal, therefore space and time are unreal. Rather the precise nature of his worries about space and time shed much light on his exact views about relations. They are a good illustration of, and may thus be used to interpret, his notoriously elusive attack on relations themselves.

Secondly, these arguments are interesting, not simply in connection with his views on relations, but also in themselves as arguments about the nature of space and time. They are not, as has sometimes been supposed, mere confusions about the correct mathematical or scientific treatment of space and time, but raise some serious points and puzzles in the philosophy of space and time to which modern mathematics or science have no easy answers.

In typically modest fashion Bradley eschews any originality with these arguments: 'The reader will be acquainted with the difficulties' (*AR* 30), he says. It is clear from what follows that Bradley has in mind two famous discussions of the nature of space and time: Kant's First and Second Antinomies in the *Critique of Pure Reason*, and the debate between substantivalism and relationism in the *Leibniz–Clarke Correspondence*.[1] The First Antinomy contrasts

---

[1] Kant (1929); Alexander (1956).

a demand that the world be finitely extended in space and time
with the demand that it be infinitely extended, while the Second
Antinomy contrasts a demand for its finite divisibility with the
demand for its infinite divisibility. The debate between substantivalism and relationism is a debate between those who see space
and time as independently existing substances and those who see
them as merely derivative of a system of spatial and temporal
relations among objects or events.

This, then, is the context of Bradley's discussion, and, as we
shall see, all of these factors play a role in Bradley's analysis of
space and time. Nevertheless, it must be added that, as is often the
case, his modesty here is also somewhat misleading, for at no
stage is he merely reiterating old objections; rather, he develops all
of these ideas and strands of argument in his own individual way.[2]
Our plan in this chapter will be to go through his arguments as
they are presented, explaining and criticizing them. In the first part
we shall examine the main argument against space. In the second
part, after briefly showing how this argument may also be applied
against time, we shall look at a second independent argument that
he gives against the reality of time. But, before we begin, it is
necessary to sound a somewhat cautionary note. Bradley's arguments here are all somewhat brief, and none is as clear or precisely
formulated as the subject-matter really requires. Thus a certain
amount of elaboration and interpretation must be expected and
allowed for.

5.1   THE UNREALITY OF SPACE

Following the style of Kant's Antinomies, the first argument is set
out in an antithetical form—that is, in the form of two contradictory theses that both force themselves upon us but neither
of which can be true. In this case the theses are that 'Space is a
relation—which it cannot be; and it is a quality or substance—
which again it cannot be' (*AR* 31). In attempting to establish each
of these two points Bradley presents two arguments, first one from
the infinite divisibility of space, and then one from the infinite
extent of space.

---

[2] Not everyone has been of this view. Swabey (1919) sees the whole chapter as
nothing more than a restatement of Kant's Second Antinomy.

5.11   *Space as Quality*

We may begin with the thesis that space is a quality or substance. What Bradley means here is a strong version of the theory of absolute space, the claim that space is something in its own right, prior to, and acting as a ground for, spatial terms and relations, rather than, as the opposing relationist view would have it, merely a system constructed out of those spatial terms and relations. He attempts to prove this by a *reductio ad absurdum* of the opposing view.

We begin with a simple claim. If space is made up of relations, these relations must have terms. Presumably, since we readily agreed with his argument in the last chapter that relations without terms are impossible, this claim will be an uncontroversial one. More problematic, on the other hand, is the question of what kind of things those terms might be.

The centre of the relationist–substantivalist debate concerns the question whether these are material or spatial terms. While the substantivalist sees spatial relations as holding between spatial terms, such as points or positions, the relationist sees them as holding between material objects, with the immediate consequence that there could be no such thing as absolute empty space. Bradley clearly favours this answer. 'Empty space', he says, '. . . is an unreal abstraction. It cannot be said to exist' (*AR* 33). To this extent Bradley might seem to be aligning himself with the relationists, but the situation is not quite as simple as that. This is only one question we might ask about the terms of spatial relations, and concerning other questions Bradley takes a decidedly substantivalist line.

Bradley's key question about the terms of spatial relations at this point is not whether they are material or not, but whether they are extended or not. Bradley's emphatic answer to this is that they must be. If we allow a spatial relation, he claims, 'The relation would join spaces' (*AR* 31)—that is, the terms of spatial relations are themselves always spatially extended. The alternative view—that the terms of spatial relations have no extension—but are mere geometrical points, he rejects. But what is wrong with this view? Many, for instance Russell,[3] have thought that it was

---

[3] Russell (1903), §419.

the correct view of space. Why does he think that the terms must be extended?

Bradley's worry is that, if the terms of the spatial relation are not extended, then it will be impossible for them to be related together to produce a whole which is extended in character, but that is of the essence of space. So, 'If the parts are not spaces, the whole is not space' (*AR* 31). This worry can be seen even more clearly for the case of time, taking duration as the analogue of extension. Bradley says, 'If you take time as a relation between units without duration, then the whole time has no duration, and is not time at all' (*AR* 33). What are we to think of this objection?

It might be thought that Bradley is expressing here the old and familiar worry about how extended space can be made up of extensionless parts. According to this argument, a finite, or even an infinite, number of extensionless points could never be added to produce a length. For, if they have no extension, the result of adding them one to another will have no length either.

This is a poor argument. It results from relying too heavily upon our ordinary intuitions about space and time, rather than the mathematical systems that we use to explain their formal properties. These are the number systems. An infinitely divisible, or continuous, space may be thought of as corresponding to the real numbers (the positive and negative fractions plus the irrational numbers), while a non-infinitely divisible, or discrete, space may be thought of as corresponding to the natural numbers (the counting numbers 0, 1, 2, 3 . . .). Using these analogies we may note two things. First, that any extended interval contains, if space is discrete, a finite number of points, and, if space is continuous, an infinite number of points. Secondly, we see that we must make a sharp distinction between extensionless points and extended intervals. The former correspond to numbers, while the latter correspond to intervals between numbers. We should not think of points as very small spatial intervals to be added up, any more than we should think of numbers as very small intervals of numbers.

Although they may not be added together in the same way as intervals, there is a clear sense in which an interval may be thought of as composed out of, or made up from, a (finite or infinite) number of such points. Just as an interval between two numbers may be given by specifying all the numbers that lie between these two, an extended interval may be given by specifying all the points that lie along that line. If we still find it hard to intuit how a (finite or infinite) number of extensionless grains can 'add up' to an extended interval, the following analogy may help. An extended patch of colour is made up of parts which are not themselves coloured. A certain arrangement of particles gives the object colour, something that the particles themselves lack. Similarly it might be thought that a series of extensionless points might together produce a whole with the property, extension, that each of its parts lacks.[4]

Since it should be clear that (reading durationless instant and enduring interval for extensionless point and extended interval) exactly the same holds for time, we see that, if this was the substance of Bradley's objection against space and time, it would indeed be a weak one. However, it is not obvious that this was his worry. The key to his real objection here is the theory of relations. His question is not how extensionless parts may be added to produce relations of extension, but the more general problem of how extensionless terms may be related together to produce extension. This can be made clear if we consider what might be called the problem of the origin of spatial metric. (The metrical properties of space are its measurable characteristics.) From where does space acquire its metrical properties?

We might begin by asking whether these come from the relations? It seems not, for a system of relations is wholly topological. (This was one of Clarke's objections in his correspondence with Leibniz.[5]) To say that A is taller than B does not tell us by how much. All we have is an ordering in space, compatible with any number of different metrics. It might be objected that relations do have quantity, in the sense that some may be multiples of others; for instance, A may be twice as far to the left of B as C. (This was Leibniz's reply.[6]) But, while this is true, it gives no measure to those intervals in terms of which all the others are given, and thus, as yet, no metric to those which are multiples of them.

This is where Bradley enters in. If relations must be internal, then their nature must be grounded in, or make a difference to, that of their terms. Applying this to the case of metrical relations, it seems the metric of the relation must derive from its terms; for

---

[4] Newton-Smith (1980), 119.
[5] Alexander (1956), 32.   [6] Ibid. 75.

instance, if A is two metres taller than B, this is, perhaps, because A is three metres and B one metre. The internality of the relation demands that the metrical character of the relation comes from its terms.

This gives us a far more powerful reason why the terms cannot be points. A point has no metric. It is an abstraction, with precisely this aspect removed, so it cannot confer it on its relations. If the terms of spatial relations were extensionless points, the relations connecting them, and thus the whole of the space which together they form, would be topological only. Instead it seems that the terms of the relations must be extended.

But how is this possible? For if, as it seems reasonable to suppose, space is infinitely divisible, the extension of a term cannot be a function of its parts, since, whatever the extension, the number of parts would be the same. This was shown by Grünbaum.[7] Were there indivisible parts to space, this might help. But it is hard to see how that can be possible, for all extension seems, at least conceptually or in thought, to be infinitely divisible.

A modern solution[8] is to say that we assign an extension by convention to a given unit. Not only is this counter-intuitive, but to Bradley it would just confirm the thesis that relational order in itself is not space, and thus that space as an essentially quantifiable thing is unreal and mere appearance.

There is, however, another kind of solution. If the terms have extension, this must be a basic quality they possess, not in virtue of their parts or the relations that compose them, but in themselves. Space or extension would then be an original or basic quality or substance, above and beyond any relations it contains. Although it may possess them, it is not reducible into parts and their relations. The internality of spatial relations forces this result upon us, thinks Bradley.

Having considered this question from the divisible side of space, Bradley turns to consider it from 'the other side'—that is to say, from the extensive aspect, considering not the parts but the whole of space. The same result follows. If it is true that the extended nature of the terms of any spatial relation is a basic quality, regardless of their divisibility, this will be no less true of the whole of space itself. Thus the whole of space also 'is a thing, or

---

[7] Grünbaum (1973), pt. I.   [8] Newton-Smith (1980), ch. 7.

substance, or quality (call it what you please), which is clearly as solid as the parts which it unites. From without, or from within, it is quite as repulsive and as simple as any of its contents' (*AR* 31).

5.12   *Space as Relation*

With this result we may turn to the opposing thesis, that space is nothing but a relation. This argument also proceeds by way of *reductio ad absurdum* of its denial. We begin by assuming that space is more than a relation, that it is a substance, and deduce an absurdity from this. The problem is that while, on the one hand, we seem forced to accept that the terms of spatial relations are intrinsically extended spaces, on the other hand, when we examine these terms, it also seems to be true that these are not indivisible, and that they may be fully expressed as themselves a system of extended parts in relations. The term breaks up in our hands. But if we look at these new parts they too are divisible into more relations and parts. Thus all we ever find is relations. Existing alone like this, separated from their terms, spatial relations seem after all to be external, and not internal.

It might be objected that Bradley is just making some sort of elementary confusion about infinity. Of course, if we divide a space *ad infinitum*, at every stage of the process the parts are still spaces, not points. In order to reach points by such a process we have to come to the end of an unending series, which is, of course, impossible. But it could be objected, as we have already seen, that this is not incompatible with our thinking of space as made up of an infinite number of points. An infinite number of points may be given all at once as making up a line, although they can never be reached by successive enumerations. Thus it might be said that Bradley was wrong to claim that we can never find any basic terms for our relations.

But, like the previous one, this objection misses the mark. Once again, the key is the theory of relations. If, as Bradley has argued, the relations must be internal, then the terms must be extended. This is not a product of how we specify them, but a demand of logic. But, in that case, because of the ever-present possibility of dividing extension, it seems that in effect internal relations demand from their terms a character incompatible with their being genuine terms. Yet, if they can have no terms, then the relations are after all external in character.

Thus thesis and antithesis both press themselves upon us. On the one hand, it is hard to see how we can understand the notion of a genuinely spatial, or metrical, relation without reference to the idea of a genuinely metrical term—the two are related internally. But, on the other hand, such terms seem to be complexes of complexes of complexes . . . , or, to put it another way, relations of relations of relations . . . , which suggests that we understand perfectly well what it is for something to be a spatial relation, even though we cannot grasp what it is for something to be a spatial term. That is to say, the relations seem, after all, to be external.

It might be suggested that Bradley's second argument fails because it does not recognize that the notion of a term is relative: to say that something is a complex of terms with respect to one relation is not to prevent its also being a simple term with respect to some other relation. Thus it is just wrong to say that we never find any terms for our relations. But it is not clear that Bradley would accept this objection. For to think of something as X with respect to Y is, for him, to consider but an unreal abstraction, and not a genuine term, in precisely the same way as to think of a billiard ball as unchanged by motion with respect to its non-spatial properties is to consider but an abstracted 'character' and not a genuine billiard ball.[9]

As with the previous thesis, Bradley then moves from considering the divisible aspect of space to considering its extensive aspect, where he argues that the same result holds good. Space, 'when taken itself as a unit', he claims, 'is essentially the reference of itself to something else' (*AR* 32). Take this unit of space. What lies outside it? There can only be more space. Thus, however large a unit we take, we never get 'more than one side of a relation to something beyond' (*AR* 32). Here it should be noted that the problem is not that we cannot find *any* terms, but that, if we take something as our term, it always engenders a new relation to an extra term. But we can never find a final term.

Here it must be admitted that Bradley's self-confessed ignorance of mathematics and geometry leads him to make a factual error. Although correct in saying that space could have no boundaries,

---

[9] See §4.22.

he takes this as equivalent to saying that 'a space limited, and yet without space that is outside, is a self-contradiction' (*AR* 32). But these are not equivalent, and the latter is not a contradiction, for in non-Euclidean space it is possible for there to be a limited space without boundaries. Formally, this is done by dropping Euclid's second postulate, that a straight line can be produced infinitely (i.e. without meeting itself again), and there are several non-Euclidean geometries, such as elliptical and spherical geometries, which do this. Intuitively, just as we may think of a circle as a finite line without ends, or a sphere as a finite plane without edges, space may be the three-dimensional analogue of this possibility (or space–time the four-dimensional analogue)—that is to say, a finite three-dimensional matrix without boundaries.

In Bradley's defence, it must be said that the application of geometry to physical space is a controversial question, and it remains unproven whether physical space is non-Euclidean in this way. Besides, our common concept of space is certainly Euclidean, so this argument could still stand as a piece of conceptual analysis of that concept. Moreover, he does not need this additional argument, if the case from divisibility still stands.

Both of these theses commend themselves and undermine the other in precisely the same way as the dialectic against terms and relations. Space is a quality, which is to say spatial relations must be internal and cannot be external. But space is nothing but a relation, which is to say that its relations must be external and cannot be internal. We oscillate between one point of view and the other, but in the end this will not do. Bradley says, 'This dilemma has been met often by the ignoring of one aspect, but it has never been, and will never be, confronted and resolved. And naturally, while it stands, it is the condemnation of space' (*AR* 31). Thus, claims Bradley, space is unreal. It is mere appearance.

5.2   THE UNREALITY OF TIME

Bradley then proceeds to use exactly the same argument against time. Since it is easy to see how this will work from the above, the details need not detain us. As before, we have an antinomy. On the one side, time is a relation—and, on the other side, it is not a relation. . . . If you take time as a relation between units without duration, then the whole time has no duration, and is not time at all. But, if you give duration to the whole time, then at once the units themselves are found to possess it; and they thus cease to be units. (*AR* 33–4)

If temporal relations are internal, not external, then their terms must possess duration; but, if their terms possess duration, then the relations must be external, not internal.

It is easy to see that the argument against time proceeds by considering time 'under a spatial form' (*AR* 33)—that is to say, by taking it to be fundamentally the same in form as space. But it is often argued that this is the wrong way to look at time, for this is not how time presents itself to us. Time, as we experience it, is not to be understood as a 'static' series of temporally related positions, but as the dynamic passage of some moving present. 'If we are to keep to time as it comes', Bradley says, 'we must confine ourselves, I presume, to time as presented' (*AR* 34). Bradley himself characterized this idea of the present in a rather graphic way in his *Principles of Logic*. He says:

Let us fancy ourselves in total darkness hung over a stream and looking down on it. The stream has no banks, and its current is covered and filled continuously with floating things. Right under our faces is a bright illuminated spot on the water, which ceaselessly widens and narrows its area, and shows us what passes away on the current. And this spot that is light is our now, our present. (*PL* 54)

It might be thought that, using this picture, time becomes immune from the previous attack, and Bradley realizes that, if he is fully to disprove time as well as space, he will have to attack this picture also. This he proceeds to do. As before, the attack consists in a dilemma that is presented to us as the result of a single question: Is this present simple or complex? Whichever way we answer, paradox follows.

The present cannot be simple, he claims, for such present moments would be but instants, and instants 'are not duration, they do not contain an after and before, and they have, by themselves, no beginning or end, and are by themselves outside of time' (*AR* 35). But then 'time becomes merely the relation between them and duration is a number of relations of the timeless, themselves also, I suppose, related somehow as to make one duration' (*AR* 35).

But neither, on the other hand, will it do to suppose (as in the theory of the specious present) that the present is complex. If it is complex, then it has extent. But, if it has extent, then it has parts, each of which could be now. But these parts themselves have parts, and thus we continue forever and are unable to find the present. 'The "now" consists of "nows", and in the end these "nows" prove undiscoverable' (*AR* 35).

To anyone familiar with the history of the philosophy of time, this argument will have a familiar sound. It is in large part a restatement of Saint Augustine's famous discussion of the present.[10] Much has been said about this argument, but it continues to exercise a great fascination over human minds. It runs as follows. How long is the present? asks Augustine. He is driven to conclude that it is but an instant, for, if it has any extension, however small, some of it must be past and some future and therefore not really present at all. But, as he rightly asks, how then can anything happen at all, for all that happens happens in the present, but the present as a meaningful scenario in which anything can happen has quite disappeared. That is to say, we have lost all sense of time as enduring.

It has been suggested that Augustine's paradox here is based upon a simple confusion. Augustine demands of the present that it be both indivisible and enduring. But this is confused, for the expression 'the present' is ambiguous between the present instant, which is indivisible but has no duration, and the present interval, which is enduring but divisible. The concepts need to be kept separate, for, although both of these demands are legitimate, that which endures and that which is indivisible are quite different things. So long as we bear this in mind, no problems need occur. On the one hand, while we are thinking of enduring intervals in which things happen, there is no need to think of the present as durationless, and hence indivisible. On the other hand, while we are thinking of indivisible instants, there is no need for us also to think of the present as enduring, and hence divisible.

While this criticism has perhaps a certain force against Augustine's statement of the argument, it fails to score against Bradley's own exposition of it. He would argue that, even if the term 'the present' is ambiguous and we must distinguish between present

---

[10] Augustine (1961), bk. XI.

intervals and present instants, since neither of these concepts on its own can provide a full account of our experience of time, we must ask how they stand to each other? But it is precisely this that we cannot explain. Each model requires, but cannot allow, supplementation from the other. Although we oscillate in our point of view from one side to the other, they cannot be combined together in a single view. Moreover, our difficulty here is not new, for it is just our old problem about terms and relations once again. Instants provide terms, but no relations for them to be terms of— that is, no duration. Enduring intervals provide relations, but no terms for the relations to hold between—that is, no instants. Thus the claim that between any two instants there is an interval is but a specific version of the thesis that between any two terms there is a relation, and, like that, explains nothing. Time cannot be a system of instants and intervals, for the same reason that reality cannot be a system of terms and relations. Hence Bradley concludes that 'Time, like space, has most evidently proved not to be real, but to be a contradictory appearance' (*AR* 36).

With subject and predicate, relation and term, and, now, space and time all shown to be contradictory and unreal, the foundations of everything else quickly collapse. But, rather than follow their demise, let us now turn to examine one of the few positive claims that Bradley has to make about reality—namely, that it is ideal.

6

Idealism and the Absolute

T H E harmonious reconciliation of difference and identity provides Bradley with the abstract skeleton or pattern which reality must possess. But there is much more to the Absolute than just this. Thus he next turns to enquire into the content of this formal structure, 'the matter which fills up [this] empty outline' (*AR* 127). About this he is unusually positive and certain. He claims that 'the Absolute is one system, and . . . its contents are nothing but sentient experience. It will hence be a single and all-inclusive experience' (*AR* 129). 'Sentient experience', he says, 'is reality, and what is not this is not real' (*AR* 127). He is then an idealist. But idealism is a broad church, so we need to enquire exactly what it is that he means by claiming that reality is experience. That enquiry is best furthered by considering the arguments that he advances in favour of this position, for the content of his claim is a direct function of his arguments for it.

But before we proceed with this task we need to consider one possible objection. It has been claimed by Cresswell that idealism, rather than something Bradley seriously argued for, needs to be seen as one of his initial and most basic assumptions. It is simply one side of his extreme empiricist view that we encounter reality only through experience or feeling (*PL* 44; *ETR* 190). Thus, although the topic is first raised by Bradley only at the beginning of book Two, Cresswell argues 'that it is the foundation and presupposition of his whole metaphysics and that the anti-relational and anti-pluralistic arguments which occur earlier in [*Appearance and Reality*] can only be understood on the assumption that we already hold the view that reality is experience'.[1]

From a literary point of view, it must be said that Cresswell's claim attributes to Bradley a very odd presentational strategy. If idealism is a necessary presupposition of the anti-relational

---

[1] Cresswell (1977) 169–70. See also Cresswell (1979). This argument has been criticized in Candlish (1981; 1982).

arguments, ought not the case for it to appear before, rather than after, them? Cresswell's thesis depends in large part on this claim that the anti-relational arguments only work if they are understood as presupposing idealism. But this, as we have seen in Chapter 4, is not the case at all: the foundations of these arguments are logical rather than epistemological. The claim that idealism was one of Bradley's basic assumptions rather than something he seriously argued for, therefore, cannot be accepted. However, Cresswell's other claim—that Bradley's idealism is intimately linked to his empiricism—is an important one. As we shall see below,[2] the belief that reality comes to us only in experience does indeed play a crucial role in Bradley's argument for idealism.

Idealist ontologies, and the arguments or motives for advancing them, are sometimes divided into two broad classes. There is objective idealism which retains, and there is subjective idealism which abandons, the distinction between how things appear and how they really are. Both of these positions will be characterized and explained in greater detail in the following two sections. The question that we need to ask here is, which, if either, of these species of idealism may be attributed to Bradley? In the following two sections I shall argue that neither of them corresponds very well to the argument that he offers, or fits in very well with the rest of his metaphysics. Instead I shall suggest, in the last section, that a careful placing of Bradley's argument for idealism in its right metaphysical context gives us a quite different picture.

6.1 OBJECTIVE IDEALISM

Objective idealism might be roughly characterized as the view that thoughts or ideas are in some sense more real than any other kind of existence, and thus that ultimate reality, however it may appear to us, is best understood as a system of ideal elements and logical connections. It is typically an ontology derived from logic rather than from epistemology, and thus anti-naturalist without being anti-realist.

Platonism and Leibnizian monadism are two other kinds of objective idealism, but the most famous version of the position,

[2] See §6.3.

and the one which has most in common with Bradley's view of the world, is undoubtedly Hegel's Absolutism.[3] Hegel thought of the world in all its detail and its history as a manifestation of rational necessity itself, whose ultimate and all-embracing expression he terms 'the Absolute Idea'. The Absolute Idea, for Hegel, is a knowing and being in one, something whose object and subject are to be understood as identical. To put the same point in a slightly different manner, he saw the universe as one simultaneously self-positing and self-conscious spirit, which embraces, but which goes beyond, every finite being. This infinite spirit he terms *Geist*.

Is Bradley's Absolute an existence of the same basic kind as Hegel's *Geist*? This would be a very natural thought, for they are similar in many respects. They are both to be understood as an infinite or unlimited spiritual entity which is unique and which can alone claim to be real. They are both to be thought of as something whose partial manifestations or appearances constitute and exhaust the world of everyday thought and experience. They are both to be seen as some kind of all-embracing self-awareness that includes, but also transcends, each finite consciousness, or self. Apparently clinching the identification, Bradley closes *Appearance and Reality* by explicitly associating his own idealism with what he says is perhaps 'the essential message of Hegel'—namely, that 'Outside of spirit there is not, and there cannot be, any reality, and, the more that anything is spiritual, so much the more is it veritably real' (*AR* 489).

Despite all these similarities, there is much room for doubt whether Hegel's Absolute idealism really provides a very good over-all model for understanding Bradley's own idealist conclusion, for there are certain aspects of Hegel's idealism which are sharply at variance with Bradley's own. This may be seen by considering the phenomenon of self-consciousness. Rational self-consciousness, for Hegel, of all the elements of finite experience, is the one that comes most close to being truly real, providing us with a special insight into the nature of reality. On the scale of reality which is set for us by the standards of logical coherence, it scores the highest. For Bradley, on the other hand, it is an appearance, contradictory like any other. His fundamental objection

---

[3] Hegel (1977).

to it is that it is relational—'Self-consciousness . . . implies a relation. It is the state where the self has become an object that stands
before the mind' (*AR* 94)—and no relational structure can provide insight into the nature of ultimate reality.

He thinks that self-consciousness is irredeemably relational because the mind of which we are conscious in this state is but an
abstraction from a wider felt background which also includes feelings, desires, and volitions. Thus self-consciousness gives us a relation between one part and the whole, not a supra-relational
unification of two different aspects of total reality, as Hegel claims.
Bradley says, 'The object is never wholly identical with the subject, and the background of feeling must contain a great deal more
than what we at any time can perceive as the self' (*AR* 94).

With this we see the root of the difference between Bradley's
and Hegel's versions of idealism. Where, for Hegel, the fundamental criterion of reality is rationality—the more a thing meets his
standards of rational or logical coherence the greater is its claim
to be real—for Bradley the relevant criteria are comprehensiveness
and self-subsistent individuality. This has the consequence that,
for Bradley, reality has to be much more than just rational thought.
Thought, for him, is but an abstraction from life, and thus something less than real. We therefore see that, despite the remarkable
surface similarities between their views, at bottom both the moti-
vation and content of Hegel's idealism were *anathema* to Bradley.
He was quite adamant about this, describing it as a 'cheap and
easy Monism' and 'an unearthly ballet of bloodless categories' (*PL*
591).

6.2 SUBJECTIVE IDEALISM

Subjective idealism might be characterized as the view that the
only direct objects of our knowledge or experience are, strictly
speaking, mental items (such as thoughts, desires, feelings, perceptions, and the like), and that there exists nothing which is not
known or experienced. In contrast to objective idealism, this kind
of anti-naturalism is usually based on epistemological and anti-
realist arguments to the effect that we can never encounter anything which is not mental, and thus that it is not reasonable—nor

perhaps even conceivable—to suppose that there should exist anything else.

There are many phenomenalists or extreme empiricists who might be said to hold such a position, but the most celebrated advocate of this kind of view is probably Berkeley. He argued that our awareness is forever limited to our own ideas, and thus that any supposed external or material universe is a hypothesis as empty as it is unfounded. Thus, for Berkeley, the only kind of existence is mental existence, a view which he expresses in the slogan, 'to be is to be perceived or to perceive'.[4]

Does this (or rather a holistic version of this, for Berkeley's universe is a pluralistic one) capture the kind of idealism that Bradley wishes to advocate? It has been thought by some critics that it does, and thus that Bradley's thought, although elsewhere often grounded in obscure logical concepts or arguments, is here surprisingly familiar, being an epistemological argument for a psychological conclusion.

In order to assess this claim, let us then take a look at Bradley's main argument for idealism. This occurs in chapter XIV of *Appearance and Reality*. At the outset it must be said that, for the magnitude of the conclusion that it attempts to establish, this argument is exceedingly compressed, covering but three pages. It is also very poorly structured. In consequence, there has been little agreement among critics about how it is supposed to work. Reconstruction is inevitable, and certainty cannot be hoped for. One thing about the argument is clear enough though. It takes the form of a Bradleian ideal experiment with the following instructions:

Find any piece of existence, take up anything that any one could possibly call a fact, or could in any sense assert to have being, and then judge if it does not consist in sentient experience. Try to discover any sense in which you can still continue to speak of it, when all perception and feeling have been removed; or point out any fragment of its matter, any aspect of its being, which is not derived from and is not still relative to this source. When the experiment is made strictly, I can myself conceive of nothing else than the experienced. (*AR* 127–8)

With respect to Bradley's idealism and this argument for it, Wollheim says that, 'In favour of this bold and obscure doctrine Bradley employs the traditional epistemological argument for

[4] Berkeley (1944), §429.

Idealism'.[5] In describing this as the traditional epistemological argument for idealism, Wollheim no doubt has in mind here Berkeley's famous conceivability argument. The arguments certainly seem to be very similar. Berkeley's argument, which occurs in *The Principles of Human Knowledge*, is an attempt to establish his immaterialist doctrine in just one simple step. It considers the response of a possible critic of the theory:

But, say you, surely there is nothing easier than for me to imagine trees, for instance, in a park, or books existing in a closet, and nobody by to perceive them. I answer, you may so, there is no difficulty in it; but what is all this, I beseech you, more than framing in *your* mind certain ideas which you call *books* and *trees*, and at the same time omitting to frame the idea of any one that may perceive them? But do you not yourself perceive or think of them all the while? This therefore is nothing to the purpose: it only shows you have the power of imagining or forming ideas in your mind; but it does not shew that you can conceive it possible the objects of your thought may exist without the mind. To make this out, it is necessary that *you* conceive them existing unconceived or unthought of, which is a manifest repugnancy.[6]

Turning to Bradley's argument, we must ask how it is supposed to work. Why is the task that he sets us supposed to be impossible? Since there is, in the literature, no general agreement about this, let us look at two different interpretations of the argument. Perhaps the most common is to read it as saying that we cannot imagine an unexperienced object because, in the very act of imagining it, we would be experiencing it, so that it was after all an experienced object. Thus the only conceivable kind of reality is experienced reality. This is how Wollheim understands the argument, and also Candlish, who glosses it thus:

Bradley invites us to try to conceive of an unexperienced object. This seems straightforward enough, until we remember that for idealists, 'experience' and 'feeling' cover all forms of psychic activity, and the instruction thus comes to 'Conceive of something unconceived'. And this description of what we are to do is plausibly regarded as either 'a mere word' or an instruction to attempt something self-contradictory or self-defeating.[7]

---

[5] Wollheim (1969), 198.   [6] Berkeley (1948–57), §23.
[7] Candlish (1984), 250. See also Wollheim (1969), 197–200.

Although that is no reason to think that Bradley was not taken in by it, along with many of his idealist contemporaries, this is a notoriously fallacious argument. The problem is that it confuses our thought itself—which is, of course, something experienced—and what that thought is of—which is, or at least claims to be, something unexperienced. To put it another way, it fails to note the distinction between what *represents* and what is *represented*, but this is the very difference which Bradley went to so much trouble to make in the first chapter of *The Principles of Logic*. What must be experienced is the sign *qua* psychological entity, but this is something quite different from the sign *qua* logical entity, or meaning.

But this interpretation of Bradley's argument may be contrasted with a quite different one which has been advocated by Sprigge. He considers that Bradley's claim needs to be taken at something far more like face value—namely, that we just do not have the ability to call anything to mind which is not experienced. Experienced things, he argues, have three distinctive kinds of properties. They have perspectival characteristics, *gestalt* organization, and (either positive or negative) aesthetic qualities. 'We are never aware of an object which does not have specific versions of each of these subject-determined qualities',[8] claims Sprigge, and nor, try as hard as we like, can we imagine one. It is for this reason that the only conceivable kind of reality is experienced reality. Clearly this argument avoids the obvious logical flaw of the previous one, but, depending as it does on a controversial claim about our abilities, which can only be established by extensive case analyses, it has only a limited power to persuade.

Can either of these reconstructions be accepted as accurate interpretations of Bradley's own argument for idealism? I shall argue that neither of them can, for two reasons. The first objection could be put like this. Both arguments result in a conclusion to the effect that it is inconceivable that there might exist anything which was not experienced. But it is hard to see quite what this conclusion can mean when we combine it with another Bradleian thesis, that there is no such thing as the experiencing self. 'In whatever way the self is taken,' says Bradley, 'it will prove to be appearance' (*AR* 103). This must be so because, being neither infinite nor

[8] Sprigge (1979), 117.

simple, it involves relations both within itself and to that which is not itself. Thus Absolute reality lies beyond any distinction between subject and object, or self and not-self. Yet how, if there are no experiencing selves, can anything, let alone everything, be experienced? The impossibility of conceiving anything that is not experienced is surely one with the impossibility of conceiving anything that is not experienced by someone, by some subject.

It is to be noted that Bradley himself does not present his conclusion as saying that everything must be *experienced*; rather he says that everything is *experience* or sentience itself. Presumably this formulation is supposed to bring out the fact that the sentience of the Absolute is not that of some experiencing self. But the change of words hardly helps us. While we think of the claim as the conclusion of some quasi-Berkelian line of reasoning, it still seems to involve a subject or self, in at least some minimal sense of these terms; but, if we think of the conclusion as characterizing something wholly beyond any distinction between subject and object, it is hard to see it as the appropriate conclusion of the argument under consideration, for that argument operates at the level of ordinary experience which is subject–object in structure. Several critics have noted this difference between the traditional way of expressing the idealist conclusion and Bradley's own formulation, and attempted to bridge the gap by treating the former as an intermediate step on the way to the latter.[9] We shall not follow them in their attempts, for I want to claim that there is an even deeper objection to this traditional epistemological way of looking at the argument, whatever the precise form of its conclusion.

The second problem is that this way of interpreting the argument attributes to it a classically anti-realist form, which as such Bradley could never accept. The basic structure of the argument is taken to be this: what we cannot conceive cannot possibly exist. But Bradley could never have accepted this, for he believes that reality is precisely other than thought, or, to be more exact, other than any thought we as finite beings could ever produce. We cannot, for instance, conceive of a supra-relational whole, but this is no reason in Bradley's eyes for doubting that one could, indeed that one must, exist. Similarly, to show that we cannot conceive of an unexperienced object would not, for Bradley, be enough to

[9] Montague (1964); Wollheim (1969); Cresswell (1977).

show that one could not exist. What is needed is an argument to the effect that anything real, *whether we can conceive it or not*, must be mental. The error of attributing this conceivability argument to Bradley comes from failing to appreciate the full realist significance of Bradley's break from Hegelian orthodoxy. He may be an idealist, but he is a strongly realist one. While he accepts that we cannot think of what is beyond thought, he 'dissent[s] wholly from the corollary that nothing more than thought exists' (*AR* 148). For this reason it seems highly misleading to think of him as belonging to the tradition of subjective idealism. Moreover, Bradley himself explicitly warns us against interpreting him in this way. He says, 'I may be supposed to urge that it [the subject] cannot transcend its own states' (*AR* 128)—just what Berkeley urges—but this, he objects, is not his claim at all.

6.3   RELATIONS AND IDEALISM

In order to arrive at the correct view of Bradley's idealism and his argument for it, it is necessary accurately to locate them within the context of his other metaphysical views. We need to bear in mind his empirical views about the primacy of feeling, as our only sure access to reality, and also his realism—that is to say, his acceptance of the transcendent nature of reality. But most importantly of all, to these we need to bring in one further factor, and that is his views about relations. Often the connection between Bradley's monism and his idealism is not fully appreciated, and these are presented as two more-or-less independent theses.[10] The correct perspective is to see that, for Bradley, idealism is in effect as direct a consequence of his views on the unreality of relations as, for example, his denial of the reality of space and time. Seen this way, although it has similarities with both objective and subjective idealism, Bradley's idealism does not really belong to either tradition.

Bradley's argument for idealism may then be reconstructed in the following way.[11] It begins with our feeling or experience. This we know is real. 'The real is that which is known in presentation

[10] Montague (1964) is a notable exception to this.
[11] A similar account of Bradley's argument may be found in Candlish (1984), §IX.

or intuitive knowledge. It is what we encounter in feeling or perception' (*PL* 44); (cf. *PL* 154–62). The claim is not yet that we know this to be the only real thing, but rather that it is the only thing we know to be real. Next it is necessary to bring in Bradley's arguments against relations. The impossibility of relations means that in the end all divisions must be overcome, and therefore feeling, like everything else finite, must go into the melting-pot. What will become of it we can hardly know, but the doctrine of relations ensures us of one thing, that it will not be lost. In the Absolute all differences are merged together, so that the whole is present in every part, and every part present in every other. Everything is inter-related. Thus ultimately there can be nothing that is wholly independent of feeling or experience.

It is true that our experience is an abstraction, and reconnecting it with the whole of reality will no doubt alter it beyond all recognition (for instance, the presence of an experiencing subject which from a limited point of view seems essential to the notion of experience in fact drops out altogether in the wider picture); but, for all that, it cannot be removed. Though the experience of the Absolute is inconceivably different from our experience, it must in all its elements be connected with it. There is nothing separate from experience, and in this sense the Absolute in all its aspects is, or implicitly involves, 'experience'. Bradley is using the term 'experience' analogically here. Though very different from ordinary experience, the entire Absolute is systematically connected and related to it, and so deserves to be designated by the same analogical term. He says:

I rest throughout on this foundation. You cannot find fact unless in unity with sentience, and one cannot in the end be divided from the other, either actually or in idea. But to be utterly indivisible from feeling or perception, to be an integral element in a whole which is experienced, this surely is itself to *be* experience. (*AR* 129)

The theory of relations tells us that everything is implicated in everything else. Thus every part of reality in its final state must be connected to experience, a full account, or analysis, of that reality in all its ramifications involving or making reference to it. Spelling out the full conditions for inclusion in the Absolute, we see that the idea of reality apart from experience is just an illegitimate abstraction. If the only reality we encounter is experience, then

We can find nothing but this, and to have an idea of anything else is plainly impossible. For such a supposed idea is either meaningless, and so is not an idea, or else its meaning will be found tacitly to consist in experience. The Other, which it asserts, is found on inquiry to be really Other. It implies, against its will and unconsciously, some mode of experience. (*AR* 463)

It is important to note the sense in which the outcome of this argument is determined by its starting-point, the existence of feeling or experience. Had we started with the existence of material objects, we would have been similarly able to argue that there was no part of the Absolute which is not material.[12] However, as things are, we start from the existence of feeling and from this move to the conclusion that everything must involve feeling, in at least some distant and analogical sense of the term. But, if everything is mental, since that excludes its also having any other nature, we can move to the further conclusion that it is *only* mental.

In this way the certainty of idealism rules out the possibility of materialism, and Bradley can conclude that 'the real is nothing but experience' (*AR* 128), although quite what kind of an experience it must be is something beyond our comprehension.

Of course, if there can be nothing which is not mental, then the extra-mental material world in which most of us believe must be something ultimately unreal, and join the ever-swelling ranks of the apparent. But, since this is such an important claim in his metaphysics, let us now turn to examine a little more closely what Bradley means when he says that things are not real, but merely apparent.

---

[12] This point is considered in Candlish (1984), 267 n. 17.

7

The Absolute
and its Appearances

WITH characteristic understatement Bradley commences the second part of *Appearance and Reality* with the words, 'The result of our First Book has been mainly negative' (*AR* 119). In this he is certainly not wrong, for, as we have seen, Bradley's philosophical system involves the condemnation of the entire world of common-sense experience and reflection.[1] Things and their properties, terms and their relations, space, and time, and the whole host of things whose analysis involves these notions are all claimed to belong, not to reality, but to the realm of appearance. This is a strange and counter-intuitive position which has not as yet been fully elucidated. We have already examined Bradley's reasons for denying the ultimate reality of these things, but what precisely does he mean by calling them 'appearance'?

The concept of 'appearance' plays a very important role in Bradley's thought; however, his use of the term is somewhat technical and idiosyncratic. None the less, we may begin in a relatively simple fashion by clearing up two potential confusions. First, it might be thought that appearances require the existence of some person or mind for them to appear to. Appearance, no less than perception, seems to be a kind of mental presentation to a conscious self. But this is problematic, for, as we have already seen, on account of the fact that they essentially involve relations, Bradley denies the reality of any such conscious selves. But in that case, what sense then can there be in talking of 'appearances'?

Secondly, it might be argued that in its original meaning the term 'appearance' applies to perception, and primarily to visual perception. For something to appear is for it to present itself (although not necessarily as it truly is) to our senses, and especially

---

[1] Not everyone has agreed with this. In so far as it takes everyday knowledge to possess a limited validity, Bradley's position has been described as 'fundamentally a philosophy of common sense' (Eliot (1975), 203).

to our sense of sight. Yet many of the phenomena that Bradley rejects as appearance are not in the least perceptual. There is no chance, for instance, of our perceiving the subject–predicate structure of reality, the self, causal connections, or space and time in themselves (as opposed to things in space and time). But what sense then can there be in calling these things 'appearances'?

Bradley addresses both of these criticisms—that appearance 'is not possible except to a percipient' and that the 'term belongs solely of right to the perceptual side of things' (*AR* 429). He admits that both objections have some substance. However, neither worry him unduly, for they merely bring out something that he himself is quite prepared to admit—namely, that he is using the term 'appearance' in a somewhat non-standard fashion. He says, 'We must, in short, admit that some appearances really do not appear, and that hence a licence is involved in our use of the term' (*AR* 430). He is making a somewhat extended use of the word.

There is, of course, nothing in principle wrong with using words in a non-standard manner, divest of some of their usual meaning and connotations, or supplemented with additional significance and implications. But likewise there is no guarantee that this is always and everywhere permissible, for the attempt may just end in nonsense. Bradley says that a certain licence is involved in his use of the term; thus the question that must be asked is whether or not we are prepared to grant him that licence, or, in other words, whether when we examine it more closely we can make any clear sense of his usage. There are reasons for doubting that we can. These were clearly expressed in 1917 by G. E. Moore,[2] whose analysis of Bradley's account of appearance will be considered in the next section.

7.1 THE PROBLEM OF APPEARANCE AND REALITY

Although Moore's attack concentrates on the specific case of time, it is in fact general in its import. What holds with regard to this particular appearance can easily be seen in the case of any other. Moore begins by noting some of the things that Bradley has to say about the reality of time. 'Time', it is claimed, 'has most evidently

---

[2] Moore (1922*a*).

proved not to be real, but to be a contradictory appearance'
(*AR* 36). Bradley denies that it 'either [has] or belong[s] to reality'
(*AR* 30). Indeed, he is prepared to stake his whole theory on this:
'If time is not unreal, I admit that our Absolute is a delusion'
(*AR* 182).

So far so good. But this group of claims he combines with
another which seems to be in direct conflict with the first. Generally, he says 'that appearances exist' (*AR* 114). To deny this, he
thinks, is nonsense, because 'what appears, for that sole reason,
most indubitably *is*; and there is no possibility of conjuring its
being away from it' (*AR* 114). But, he says, 'whatever exists must
belong to reality', for, he continues, 'It has a positive character
which is indubitable fact, and, however much this fact may be
pronounced appearance, it can have no place in which to live
except reality' (*AR* 114). The general point is borne out in the
specific case for time. Though an appearance, it none the less does
exist, and therefore must 'in some way belong to our Absolute'
(*AR* 181), that is, to reality.

The problem is that these two groups of claims seem to be
straightforwardly incompatible with each other, for in effect Bradley
appears to be claiming both that 'Time is not real and does
not belong to reality', and that 'Time is real and does belong to
reality'.

Of course, Bradley does not think it fatal to his theory to maintain
both of these groups of claims, and Moore goes on to consider
some reasons why not. But, before we turn to consider Bradley's
solution to this apparent paradox, it would be well for us to make
a detour and place the specific problem in its wider significance.
This is the puzzle of how appearance in general is related to
reality, for, although we have limited our discussion to one particular appearance, time, it is clear that the same problem arises
for all. What then is the relationship between reality and appearance in general?

As was noted in an important and unjustly neglected paper by
Foster,[3] to anyone who has worked through *Appearance and Reality*
from the beginning, this problem will have a particularly paradoxical force. We have asked how appearance is related to reality,
but, in view of the central thesis that all relations are unreal, the

[3] Foster (1930).

more serious problem is to see how they can be related at all. There is no coherent means of connecting them, yet neither is it coherent to suppose that they be wholly unconnected. Exactly the same problem that we encountered at the everyday level now appears at the meta-level. Bradley seems to be caught on his own hook. Sometimes he sees the connection between appearance and reality as a relation (*AR* 488), sometimes more specifically as a predication (*AR* 430). But these devices are no more satisfactory here than they were before, and this is something that Bradley explicitly recognizes, accepting that, strictly speaking, there can be no relations at this higher level between appearance and reality (*AR* 285 n.).

The effect of the problem is dramatic. At the everyday level, the attempt to think out relations or predications led to a helpless oscillation between identity and difference: first P is thought of as identical with S, and then they are taken to be quite distinct. But now we find precisely the same oscillation repeated at the meta-level: on the one hand, the Absolute is identical with the sum of its appearances (*AR* 405), but, on the other hand, the Absolute is separate from its appearances (*AR* 413). Statements about the relationship between appearance and reality oscillate between these two alternatives. The contradiction that Moore has noted in the specific case of time, that it is both a part of reality and distinguished from reality, is merely one particular instance of this general oscillation.

7.2 PHENOMENALISM AND THINGS-IN-THEMSELVES

But, if this oscillation is unacceptable and contradictory at the everyday level, it is no less so at the meta-level. There are two positions: either to identify or to distinguish reality and its appearances. But Bradley is unable to accept either of these positions. Indeed, they are both explicitly rejected in the last two chapters of the first part of the book, in the form of the two philosophical doctrines of phenomenalism and Kantian transcendentalism.

On the one hand, we might think that reality is no more than the sum of its appearances. This would be the view of phenomenalism. Phenomenalism is the theory that all that exists is phenomena (where these are understood as perhaps feelings or sensations), and the ways in which these are related or arranged together. Objects, such as things and selves, exist merely as collections or arrangements of such presented elements, while natural laws are mere dictums telling us that, when we have certain things given, then certain other things may or will be given as well.

While accepting that phenomenalism has a legitimate and even a necessary place in the realm of science,[4] Bradley argues that, as a doctrine of fundamental metaphysics, it is quite untenable (*AR* 109). He raises a number of objections against the theory. His primary and 'fatal objection' (*AR* 106) is that phenomenalism as a theory of the world is radically incomplete, for it is unable to give any account of the unity that we are able to introduce into the world by thinking. How is it that certain elements come together to form a single thing? What does its identity consist in if there exists nothing more than these elements? All such unity is a mystery to the theory. Even the unity of the theory itself defeats it, for the theory itself possesses a unity and integration of a kind not allowed for within its own strictures. Following from this are a number of attendant problems; how, for instance, are we to account for change, identity, or the necessitating character of scientific laws? So long as we are restricted to phenomena and their actual connections, there can be no explanation of essence, unity, or necessity, and hence no science, but to offer any such deeper explanations is to go beyond the merely presented phenomena and become a transcendent metaphysics. For this reason then it is quite untenable to suppose that reality is no more than the sum of its appearances.

On the other hand, we might distinguish reality from its appearances. Since all that we ever encounter falls within the realm of appearance, this would give us a Kantian model of phenomena and noumena. According to this familiar view, the universe divides into two quite different regions. On the one hand, we have phenomena, or things as they appear to us, the region of all our knowledge and experience. Set against this, on the other hand, we have noumena, or things as they are in themselves, a quite unknowable region of which we can have no knowledge or experience whatsoever.

In common with other philosophers of a Hegelian persuasion,

---

[4] Mander (1991), 70–2.

Bradley finds this theory to be wholly self-contradictory. If the noumenal realm was really unknowable, then we could never know that it existed. The doctrine is in some fundamental sense self-defeating, for there is no reconciling any knowledge of the truth of the theory with the conditions that in fact obtain if it is true. We are offered the following analogy: it is as though I were to lament that, because my faculties are confined to my garden, I cannot tell whether or not the roses in the next-door garden are in flower. If my faculties really are confined to my garden, I cannot tell whether or not there is a *garden* next door (*AR* 111). Bradley concludes that 'The assertion of a reality falling outside knowledge, is quite nonsensical' (*AR* 114).

Lest it be thought that Bradley's own theory transgresses this rule, we should note the precise way in which it is formulated, for, while he does not believe in a reality outside what he calls knowledge, he does, as we have already seen, believe in a reality outside thought. And, although this reality cannot be thought, it can, he thinks, be known or located as the limit towards which thought tends. This is a crucial distinction, upon which Bradley's entire philosophy might be said to stand or fall. It is by this means that he believes himself able to steer a path between the Charybdis of a Hegelian identity between thought and reality and the Scylla of a Kantian dualism.

Bradley also offers a further objection to the Kantian theory, which is particularly relevant to our discussion here. According to this theory we have appearance on the one side and reality on the other; but how, he asks, are these supposed to stand to each other? There are only two possible answers, and both, he claims, are equally fatal to the theory. One possibility is that the thing in itself stands in some sort of relation to its appearances, but then it is hard to avoid the conclusion that it is in some sense qualified by them, and hence no longer unknowable. Alternatively, they are not related, but then the thing in itself either has qualities or it does not. If it does, we have merely doubled our problems by reintroducing the very troubles we sought to escape, yet, if it is unqualified, then it is far from clear in what sense it can still claim to be real (*AR* 112).

For these reasons, then, Bradley believes that the Kantian model must be rejected, and that, although we cannot take reality as an aggregate made up of all its appearances, it must be regarded as equally untenable to suppose that reality is something other than, or distinct from the sum of, its appearances.

7.3 DEGREES OF TRUTH AND REALITY

Thus neither Kantianism nor phenomenalism is an acceptable position; yet it seems that we are compelled to oscillate between asserting both. We have to claim both that 'No appearance, nor any combination of these, is the same as Reality' (*AR* 430) and that 'The Absolute *is* its appearances' (*AR* 431). What is to be done? Is there no way between what Bradley calls 'this empty transcendence and this shallow Pantheism' (*AR* 488)? He claims that there is, and that the answer to our problem is to be found in the theory of the degrees of truth and reality (*AR* 431). In order to assess this claim we shall first give a simple exposition of the theory and then consider some objections and offer a critical opinion of it.

7.31 *Exposition of the Theory*

What is this theory, and how does it work? Bradley claims that in developing it he was heavily indebted to Hegel (*AR* 318 n.). In order to understand the theory we must first briefly remind ourselves of Bradley's conception of thought and judgement. An idea or thought is an abstracted part or aspect of reality considered apart from its existence, and judgement the act which refers this ideal content to a reality beyond that act. There are two further things that need to be added to this. First, although the ideal content has its own complexity, it functions as a single idea. This means that the subject of the judgement must lie outside of it and is reality as a whole. We judge not that 'S is P' but that 'Reality is such that S is P'. Secondly, all judgements are hypothetical in the sense of carrying with them the implicit conditions of their application. 'Judgements are conditional in this sense, that what they affirm is incomplete. It cannot be attributed to Reality, as such, and before its necessary complement is added' (*AR* 320). So the final form of our judgement is 'Reality is such that if $C_1 \ldots C_n$ then S is P'. The addition or subtraction of these conditions alters the contained judgement. Thus by filling in these implicit conditions we reach the final goal of judgement—namely, an identity with reality. This provides us with all the necessary material for understanding the theory of degrees of truth and reality. This theory may be presented in the form of three theses.

The first thesis of the theory is that no judgement is ever wholly true, but all are to some extent false. Thought is a limited abstraction from reality, and, in order to bring it closer to the truth, we must lessen the amount of difference between it and reality. This is done by filling in the implicit conditions under which the abstraction was made. But, however much we do this, we can never reach ultimate truth, for there is one last condition which can never be filled. Ultimate truth would involve its complete identity with reality, but it is the very essence of thought to be abstracted from reality (to separate content from existence). Thus thought's attempt to reach ultimate truth

would in the end be suicidal. Truth should mean what it stands for, and should stand for what it means; but these two aspects in the end prove incompatible. There is still a difference, unremoved, between the subject and the predicate, a difference which, while it persists, shows a failure in thought, but which, if removed, would wholly destroy the special essence of thinking. (*AR* 319)

Another way of putting this same point would be to say that thought, being essentially relational in nature, can never reach the Absolute, which is supra-relational in nature.

The second thesis of the theory is that no judgement is ever wholly false, but all are to some extent true. Just as there could be no judgement which fulfilled all the conditions of its application, equally there could be no judgement which failed to fulfil any of them. If the complete truth of a judgement consists in the identity of its ideal content with reality, the complete falsehood of a judgement must consist in their total diversity. But this too is impossible, for the ideal content of a judgement is not something quite separate from reality, but merely an abstraction from it, and thus always belonging to it in some respect or other, and always applicable to it under some condition or other. 'A total error', says Bradley, 'would mean the attribution of a content to Reality, which, even when redistributed and dissolved, could still not be assimilated. And no such extreme case seems possible' (*AR* 323). In some form or other, the content of the judgement must be attributable to reality as a whole.

But what, it might be objected, about contradictions or purely imaginary judgements? The simplest answer to this problem would be for Bradley to respond that such things fall outside the scope of his theory because they are not really referred to reality, and so are not even candidates for truth and falsity. However, he is unwilling to take this solution. To explain why, it is necessary to develop a little further Bradley's theory of judgement. In the brief resumé above, we first presented Bradley's notion of an idea or sign, and then described his conception of judgement as the way in which these ideas are used to refer to reality. This conforms to the way in which he first presented the matter in *The Principles of Logic*. However, Bradley grew increasingly sceptical of this way of seeing things. He was particularly suspicious of its implication, exploited in the strategy that we suggested above, that there could be ideas which simply floated before the mind without being applied to reality in the form of a judgement. Pressure to abandon this aspect of his theory came from outside, and especially from Bosanquet, who, in his *Logic*, urged that we should think of concepts 'as existing only in the act of judgement'. 'Ideas and impressions . . . are not found lying apart as words lie on a page', he objects; only 'by a reflective abstraction' can we so regard them as lying about.[5] But there was also internal pressure from Bradley's own system—for instance, from his strongly anti-abstractionist stance. The whole notion that we can, without distortion, remove the content from the act of judging runs counter to this holism.

By the time of *Appearance and Reality* the position was abandoned and Bradley held that there could be no abstraction of ideas from some reality which was not at the same time a judgement, or reference of them to some other reality. 'Every idea, used as an idea, must so far attach itself as an adjective to the real, and hence in the end there will be no such thing as an idea which merely floats' (*ETR* 29). In the end every symbol or idea is referred to reality, as a symbol or idea of something—for this is part of what it means to be such a sign—and thus whatever occurs as a symbol is, by that very fact, present in an act of judgement.[6]

But this means that we still have to face the previous objection

[5] Bosanquet (1911), 32.
[6] An additional consequence of this view is that, since all judgements must be placed within their psychological context of the act of judging, they must all be intensional or referentially opaque. See Allard (1985).

to the doctrine that no judgement is wholly false—namely, that there are certain notions (such as the imaginary or the contradictory) for which it is hard to see how any reference in reality could be found. It should be noted that the denial of floating ideas in itself does not produce this problem, but only in combination with the additional thesis that no judgement is ever wholly false. Bradley's solution to the difficulty is as simple as it is daring; we must simply expand the realm of possible reference.

Thus we arrive at what we might call his many-worlds doctrine. The problem, thinks Bradley, is that we operate with a false and unduly narrow assumption as to the limits of reality. He argues that the world we all call the 'real world' is no more than an abstracted construction on our part, in that it is but a fragment of a much wider reality. We abstract out a part of that reality, essentially no more than whatever is to be found in 'continuous connexion with [our] felt waking body' (*ETR* 30), but it is no more than a part, and there are always other parts, or 'other worlds', that we could abstract. Some may be subsets of our waking world, others may intersect with it, and yet others wholly transcend it. There are, claims Bradley, an indefinite number of such worlds. He lists some of them. There are the worlds of politics, or commerce, those of religion, or duty, those of art, or imagination, and even those of dreaming (*ETR* 31).

All of these realms (like 'our own real world') are in some sense unreal, for none is identical with the Absolute, which, while it includes, also transcends, them all. None the less, they are real enough to function as references for ideas which are not immediately attributable to our waking world. Thus no idea need ever float in any final sense. Although it may qualify nothing in the everyday world, it will always qualify some other world. This then is one part of what Bradley means when he says that, with suitable reinterpretation, no idea could ever fail to qualify some aspect or other of reality, and what allows him to retain his thesis that no judgement is wholly false, but that all are somehow true.

Thus every thought is true, but none wholly so, and every thought is false, but none wholly so. The final piece of the theory is to see that this is a matter of degree:

with this we have arrived at the meeting-ground of error and truth. There will be no truth which is entirely true, just as there will be no error which is totally false. With all alike, if taken strictly, it will be a question of amount, and will be a matter of more or less. (*AR* 320-1)

Abstractions from reality can only be reapplied to it subject to a host of conditions discounting the effects of the abstraction. Filling these in alters the predicate. Thus, as a measure of the degree of truth, we can ask how much conversion would be required to turn a false abstraction into absolute truth. Or equivalently, since the completion of conditions alters the assertion, we can ask how much of the original assertion would survive if we convert it into absolute truth. 'The amount of survival in each case . . . gives the degree of reality and truth' (*AR* 323).

Finally, we need to consider the claim that this is a theory of degrees of reality as well as a theory of degrees of truth. That it should be a theory of both follows directly from Bradley's view of the relationship between logic and metaphysics, between which, it will be remembered, there is no fundamental distinction of subject-matter. Lest this should seem more strange than it is, we should note right away that 'The Absolute, considered as such, has of course no degrees; for it is perfect, and there can be no more or less in perfection. . . . Such predicates belong to, and have meaning only in the world of appearance' (*AR* 318). The idea is that we may take anything and measure its degree of reality by the extent of its coherence and comprehensiveness—the extent to which it approximates the complete coherence and comprehensiveness of the Absolute. But, since outside limitation is a defect, and completing this would of necessity alter it, 'you may measure the reality of anything by the relative amount of transformation, which would follow if its defects were made good' (*AR* 332).

7.32   Criticism of the Theory

With this brief account of the doctrine of degrees of truth and reality behind us, let us now turn to the question of assessing its merits. What are we to make of this theory? The notion that there might be degrees of truth is certainly a strange one, for it is normally thought that there are only two truth-values. In order to see whether it can be sustained, let us consider (in something like order of severity) a number of criticisms that could be made against it.

First, it might be objected that degrees of truth are incompatible with classical formal logic, and its theorems, such as the law of excluded middle, as standardly understood. This is certainly true, but hardly in itself a reason to reject the theory, for the question is precisely whether or not we should abandon classical formal logic. Nor is the problem one of having to abandon formalism altogether, for there exist alternative systems of symbolic logic quite capable of representing degrees of truth. Formal models with three or more truth-values are familiar to most people, and it is a short step from that to a logic with denumerably many truth-values, represented perhaps by some real number between 0 and 1. Within such systems we may even formulate acceptable analogues of the classical laws of logic, such as the law of excluded middle. The key question concerns how we should interpret these models, and consequently whether or not we should be tempted to abandon classical logic for them.

A second objection to the theory is that it is somehow self-refuting. If nothing is wholly true, then neither Bradley's metaphysics nor indeed his theory of truth can be wholly true. Yet he seems to be claiming that they are. There certainly seems to be some warrant in this last claim, for Bradley clearly accepted that, in doing metaphysics, it is necessary to treat certain principles as absolutely true. That, as Bradley puts it, is the rule of the game.

Thinking is the attempt to satisfy a special impulse, and the attempt implies an assumption about reality. You may avoid the assumption so far as you decline to think, but, if you sit down to the game, there is only one way of playing. In order to think at all you must subject yourself to a standard, a standard which implies an absolute knowledge of reality; and while you doubt this, you accept it, and obey while you rebel. (*AR* 134–5)

But such a position would certainly seem to contradict the theory of degrees of truth and reality. This charge was raised by Russell. Taking the form of the theory which says that all truths are partial, he objects that, 'if no partial truth is quite true, then it cannot be quite true that no partial truth is quite true', and nor can any philosophical theory which supports it. But, if the philosophy which supports the view is not itself quite true, 'it may be that the elements . . . which require correction, are just those which are essential to establishing [this] view of truth'.[7]

[7] Russell (1906–7), 30.

Does Bradley make this mistake? I do not think it can be said that he does. Elsewhere he is more clear about the precise nature of these absolute principles. They are only truths which, 'for the present at least, we can regard as unconditional' (*AR* 480). We accept any such truth, not because it is absolutely true or incorrigible—no truth has that status—but because it 'is not *intellectually* corrigible. There is no intellectual alteration which could possibly, as general truth, bring it nearer ultimate Reality' (*AR* 483). He makes a relative distinction between absolute and finite truths. Both are conditioned and depend for their truth upon something not included within the judgement, but the former, which include the truths of metaphysics, are as general as judgements can possibly be, and thus unconditioned by anything within thought itself. He says, 'Absolute truth is corrected only by passing outside the intellect. It is modified only by taking in the remaining aspects of experience. But in this passage the proper nature of truth is, of course, transformed and perishes' (*AR* 483). They are thus as true as any judgements could ever be. This solves the problem. While it would certainly be contradictory to claim absolute truth for the thesis that there is no absolute truth, there is no contradiction in claiming that that thesis is as true as any could ever be. If we are to think at all, we have to use judgements and axioms and to treat them as true. This is perfectly reasonable if they are the truest ones possible. Russell's mistake is to infer from the fact that the truth is not quite true to the fact that it permits correction.

A third, quite different, criticism of Bradley's doctrine of degrees of truth would be to ask why we should think of these as degrees of truth at all, rather than degrees of epistemic warrant or utility? What, it might be asked, is the difference between saying that one proposition is more true than another, and saying simply that it possesses a greater epistemic warrant or is more useful? It was precisely this question that formed the centre of Bradley's long controversy with the pragmatists. Against the pragmatists, Bradley claims that, although differing degrees of truth may in fact be correlated with differing levels of utility, they are not to be identified with them. In claiming that propositions are only more or less true, he insists that he does not mean simply that, 'for working purposes, our judgements are admissible and will pass. I mean that less and more they actually possess the character and type of absolute truth and reality' (*AR* 321).

The crucial difference between Bradley and the pragmatists here is that, for Bradley, truth is a transcendent notion. To his way of thinking, the final truth of a thought involves the transcendence and dissolution of that thought itself into the Absolute. Hence it cannot be defined in terms of epistemic virtues (such as warranted assertability or utility), not even if (as with the modern-day internal realists[8]) we take the step of idealizing or extending those virtues. The debate over whether or not the nature of truth should be understood as transcendent of thought is very old, and not one into which we can enter here. But it should be clear that, if we accept that truth has in fact such a nature, then degrees of truth may easily be seen as a measure of a judgement's progress along this route to self-transcendence, and thus of a fundamentally different category from degrees of epistemic soundness.

By way of a fourth criticism, it might be objected that, even if the relationship between thought and reality is as Bradley urges, we should just preserve traditional philosophical usage and reserve the term 'truth' for the highest rank, calling anything else which is not thus 'true', 'false'. While this would indeed have the virtue of conserving standard philosophical use, it is not immediately clear why it should be preferred over the alternative of introducing a scale, for there is a sense in which the latter is closer to ordinary usage. We seem to be presented with a choice. How might a decision be made? The problem seems analogous to the following. Imagine that you have just marked an exam for which 100 per cent is needed to pass. Should you publish the results for each examinee as pass or fail, or as a percentage? What reasons might be given for a choice in this case? The relevant considerations seem to be of two different sorts.

One would concern the purpose of publishing the results. If all that matters is passing or failing, then the grades are unnecessary. But clearly there are other possible situations in which it could also be important to know how close or far you were from success. This certainly seems to be the case with truth. It is not a general epistemic principle that a miss is as good as a mile. If what we say misses the mark of absolute truth, then we generally want to know where and how significant our errors were.

The second kind of consideration which is relevant to a decision concerns the feasibility of publishing the different kinds of results.

[8] Putnam (1981).

It may be that, while we can detect a perfect exam paper, there is no reliable way to compare different papers which are less than perfect. In such a case the results would have to be published as pass and fail only. There is a certain similarity between this case and the situation with truth. While we all recognize an intuitive sense in which one statement may be more true than another, it turns out to be very difficult to express this in a sufficiently precise or formal way to act as the basis for a plausible theory of degrees of truth.

There can be no denying the intuitive sense in which we may find one statement truer than another. 'All swans are white', though not true, seems truer than 'All swans are green'. This intuitive sense is available on any of the traditional theories of truth: between two statements, one could correspond better to reality, one could be more useful, or one could cohere with a wider range of propositions. Bradley's theory of truth is no different in this respect: one could require less alteration to turn it into reality.

This is all very well, but insufficiently precise to ground a *theory* of truth degrees. However, when we leave behind our intuitive sense and attempt to formulate something more precise, the matter collapses in our hands. While a scale model of some object with the wrong colours is perhaps less true than the same scale model with the right colours, things are rarely as easy as that. Consider a full-size replica of some object but with the wrong colours, and a scale model with the correct colours. Which is more true? None of the traditional theories of truth can help us here. How does failure to correspond in colour rank next to failure to correspond in size? Which is more useful? Which has the wider range of coherence? We cannot answer. Nor is Bradley's theory any superior in this respect. Which would cause less change in the object, correcting the colour or correcting the size? Again, it is impossible to answer. The problem is that there are a multitude of ways a statement may succeed or fail to express the truth, and we have no common measure by which to compare them. But, until we possess such a measure, multi-valued truth systems will never rank as serious competitors to bivalent systems. For this reason I think it must be said that Bradley has failed to provide us with a theory of degrees of truth capable of going beyond our merely intuitive sense of the matter, and thus capable of challenging the traditional conception.

A fifth, and last, worry about this theory concerns the fact that, as well as being a theory of degrees of truth, it is also a theory of the differing degrees of reality possessed by the various appearances of the Absolute. Even more than differing degrees of truth, that there should exist differing degrees of reality is something that we find very counter-intuitive. None the less, on Bradley's system, the position clearly must follow. If ideas, being abstractions from reality, can be more or less true, that is, more or less advanced along the route of becoming identical with reality, then the same must hold true of appearances. This is because appearances are also abstractions from reality, and thus also capable of being assessed by the degree to which they approximate that reality. Degrees of reality can therefore be given a fairly well-defined sense, and may be thought of as the amount of transformation that would be required to turn any appearance into the Absolute. An equivalent definition is the degree of coherence and comprehensiveness possessed by any aspect of reality taken in isolation from the whole.

In spite of this, the idea remains counter-intuitive. We have a natural presupposition that reality is not a degree notion. If something exists, it is real, and, if it does not exist, it is not real, and that is all there is to it. Moreover, there are times when Bradley himself appears to use the word in this fashion. These instances, and the ambiguity which explains them, will be explored in the next section, but for an immediate example it is sufficient to note that throughout the whole of the first part of *Appearance and Reality*, in which every aspect of the common-sense world in turn is dismissed as unreal, only once is it ever suggested that this condemnation may be a matter of degree.[9]

7.4   A SOLUTION TO THE PROBLEM?

How does the theory of the degrees of truth and reality help us to solve the problem of the relationship between appearance and reality? This may be seen most clearly if we return to Moore's

---

[9] Foster ((1930), 48) and Acton ((1967), 362) claim that he *never* suggests that this condemnation is less than total. But that is not quite correct. The conclusion of his attack on personal identity is expressed thus: 'The self is no doubt the highest form of experience which we have, but, for all that, is not a true form' (*AR* 103). This suggests that it is less unreal than some other appearances.

discussion of the point. Moore's objection was that, with reference to the specific case of time, Bradley seemed to be contradicting himself and saying both that it is unreal and that it is real. Moore points out that there are two (not necessarily exclusive) ways of escaping this conclusion. One possibility is that Bradley is equivocating on different senses of the word 'time', so that what the two claims really amount to are that time in one sense is unreal whereas time in another sense is real. Alternatively, we might suppose that he is equivocating on different senses of the word 'real', so the two claims are that time is real in one sense, but unreal in another sense. The theory of degrees of truth and reality tries to solve the problem of the relationship between appearance and reality by simultaneously taking both routes.

As part of the solution we have an equivocation on different senses of the word 'time'. To begin with there is time as it appears to us. This is but an abstraction from reality as a whole, and, according to Bradley, if we replace it in its wider context, it passes beyond itself and is changed in nature by inclusion of its relations to that context, yielding a quite different kind of time. Putting these facts into the equation, our two problem sentences might be rewritten '(Abstracted) time is not real' but '(Contextualized) time is real', and the contradiction avoided. Further light can be shed on to the case by considering an analogy with a quality such as colour. If someone says that colour is unreal, this may mean that there exists nothing in bodies like the colour of phenomenal experience. But, if so, to say this is compatible with saying that colour is real in at least this sense: our experience is no mere illusion or dream, for there exists in bodies some property (or set of properties) both necessary and sufficient to cause, and in fact responsible for causing, our experience of colour. Thus colour is real; it simply does not appear to us in the way that it exists in itself. The potential contradiction is avoided by distinguishing between phenomenal and real colour.

There is no doubt that at times Bradley avails himself of this escape route. In the case of time, he denies that, 'in the character which . . . [it] exhibits[s] . . . [it] either . . . [has or belong[s] to reality' (*AR* 30), which suggests that in some other character it is real. This is borne out a little later on. 'Time is not real as such', we are told, yet on the other hand it does belong to a higher reality, and 'Its own temporal nature does not there cease wholly to exist but is thoroughly transmuted' (*AR* 185). Again, 'The Absolute is timeless, but it possesses time as an isolated aspect, an aspect which, in ceasing to be isolated, loses its special character' (*AR* 185). In other words, (contextualized) time, though including (abstracted) time, transcends it and becomes something quite different.

But this is not all that there is to Bradley's solution. In claiming that time is both real and not real, he is also equivocating on the word 'real'. When he claims that things are not real or true, what he means is that they are not absolutely real or absolutely true. But when he insists that they are none the less real or true, what he means is that they do at least possess some degree of truth or reality. Thus the two claims are to be read, 'Time is not (fully) real' and 'Time is (partially) real', avoiding any contradiction between them.

Again there can be no doubt that Bradley is availing himself of this response as well. Although not possessed of ultimate and final reality, time does exist, and is therefore endowed with a level of reality proportionate to its nature as appearance. Appearances are either real or unreal depending on the level from which you look at them. Bradley says:

Everything is essential, and yet one thing is worthless in comparison with others. Nothing is perfect, as such, and yet everything in some degree contains a vital function of Perfection. Every attitude of experience, every sphere or level of the world, is a necessary factor in the Absolute. Each in its own way satisfies, until compared with that which is more than itself. Hence appearance is error, if you will, but not every error is illusion. At each stage is involved the principle of that which is higher, and every stage (it is therefore true) is already inconsistent. But on the other hand, taken for itself and measured by its own ideas, every level has truth. It meets, we may say, its own claims, and proves false only when tried by that which is already beyond it. And thus the Absolute is immanent alike through every region of appearances. There are degrees and ranks, but, one and all, they are alike indispensable. (*AR* 431)

It is clearly possible to combine both of these parts to the solution. In that case our two claims now read, '(Abstracted) time is (partially) real' and '(Contextualized) time is (fully) real', removing their incompatibility. Thus the theory of the degrees of truth and reality may be used to solve our original problem, by distinguishing between the different levels of reality possessed by correspondingly different levels of appearances. As the appearances become more and more transmuted by inclusion of the remainder of reality, they increase in degree of reality. In this way reality is both identified with and distinguished from its appearances. 'The Absolute, we may say in general, has no assets beyond appearances; and again, with appearances alone to its credit, the Absolute would be bankrupt. All of these are worthless alike apart from transmutation' (*AR* 433).

This then is Bradley's solution to the problem of the relationship between thought and reality. While it certainly seems to work on paper, we have to ask whether the theory really represents a successful solution to our original problem? In view of Foster's points, it would be most surprising if it did, for, by Bradley's own principles, the problem is insoluble. It will be remembered that Bradley did not believe that the ordinary level problems of subjects and predicates and of terms and relations were soluble in thought, but only in a realm beyond thought. Any account that we offer is but a makeshift or metaphor, with no theoretical validity. But if this is the case at the ordinary level, why should things be any different at the meta-level?

And indeed, when we take a closer look at the theory, we see that it does begin to break apart under its own internal tensions. Despite his officially stated position, Bradley finds himself pulled in opposing directions. While distinctions can be made between (abstracted) appearances and (contextualized) ones, or between (absolute) reality and (partial) reality, throughout much of *Appearance and Reality* these distinctions are given a relatively minor role, while other less harmonizing factors take over.

One of these concerns a rather unwelcome implication of the term 'appearance'. This is that an appearance must be an appearance of something—for instance, a circle appears to be oval shaped, or a straight stick appears to be bent. But what are Bradleian appearances appearances of? They are not appearances of the Absolute in its entirety, for that is something more than any one of its appearances, yet to say they are appearances of the relevant part of the absolute is simply to repeat oneself and say they are appearances of themselves. But the point of calling them appearances in this connection is precisely that they are not faithful representations of anything as it is in itself. And to say that we do not know what they are appearances of is to embrace a

Kantian-style solution. The problem is that by drawing out this unwelcome implication of a contrast between appearances and what they are appearances of, Bradley's thought is inevitably drawn towards the kind of answer that distinguished appearances and reality, and one horn of the dilemma we had hoped to avoid.

But this is not his only problem. Bradley's insistence that, despite the shortcomings of appearances, we cannot reject any portion of reality is sometimes expressed in the following way. He says, 'appearances exist. That is absolutely certain, and to deny it is nonsense . . . What appears, for that sole reason, most indubitably *is*; and there is no possibility of conjuring its being away from it' (*AR* 114). Moreover, in making this claim, he is not saying something that applies to, for instance, (contextualized) time as opposed to (abstracted) time. He is not simply claiming that, if not in 'the character which it exhibits', then at least in some other character, time exists. Rather his point is that time, even in the character which it exhibits, exists and indubitably is. But this is a problem. Since we are told that reality encompasses all that exists, it seems reasonable to take reality and the sum of all that exists as equivalent notions. But, since we are also told that nothing exists apart from appearances, this carries the unwelcome implication that reality is the sum of all its appearances. But now we are being pushed in the opposite, and equally unwelcome, direction of identifying appearances and reality, the second horn of the dilemma that we had hoped to avoid.

Thus we see that, in spite of Bradley's reconciling theory of degrees of truth and reality, the whole book is shot through with tendencies that pull in opposite directions. Indeed at the very same time as he is putting it forward, the theory is falling apart under the strain of these forces, and it is thereby exposed as the unwieldy and ad hoc attempt to weld together the two unsatisfactory but fundamentally opposing answers of phenomenenalism and Kantianism that it really is. This should come as no surprise.

There is one final question that needs to be asked. Is the fact that this theory is shown to be unstable a problem for Bradley? It seems to me that it is not. Indeed it is to be expected. The way to understand this is to see the precise sense in which Bradley calls it a solution. At the everyday level the solution to our problem lies in a realm beyond thought, which can only be pointed at, or gestured towards, in pictures or metaphors. These function as suggestions or makeshifts, and are for that reason quite indispensable, but they have no theoretical validity whatsoever. The situation is no different at this more general level. We can never accurately express, nor indeed even think of, the ultimate connection between appearance and reality, but merely point towards it. Bradley employs many devices with this aim in view. He speaks of absorption, transmutation, transformation, merging, dissolution, and many other similar ideas (*AR* 199, 432, 332, 406, 323). He even speaks of appearances as qualifying, or related to, reality (*AR* 167, 488). But none of these is to be taken literally. And the case is no different with the doctrine of degrees of truth and reality. If he calls it a theory or a solution to the problem, it is only because it might be said to contain more information than the other metaphors which he gives. But, although it contains more information, it is no less a metaphor or pointer towards something which, although theoretically compelling, is ultimately inexpressible. Taking it this way is unavoidable; indeed to take it in any other way would be to contradict Bradley's fundamental position, for it would be to take him to be thinking of a solution which lies only beyond thought.

Whether we can accept this solution is, of course, another matter, for not without some justification might it be rejected as either empty or mysterious. However, to reject Bradley's account of the relation between appearance and reality, or even to raise this relationship as a problem for him, would not be to locate any new problem within his metaphysics. There is no more reason to reject his solution, or consider the problem to be fatally insoluble, here than there is in the case of everyday relations that we met earlier.

8
System and Scepticism

IN this last chapter I want to turn to some general questions concerning the interpretation of Bradley's philosophy. If we examine the range of critical opinions, we find that there are a number of issues in Bradley's philosophy on which there exist a polarity of interpretative viewpoints. Most of these should be familiar from the foregoing study, but let us review some of them.

8.1 THE MEETING OF TWO TRADITIONS

To begin with, there is the question of who were his main influences. While some cite the German idealists, and those such as Stirling, Caird, and Green[1] who introduced their ideas into England, others stress more strongly the influence of metaphysical realists, such as Lotze, Sigwart, Wundt, and Herbart,[2] as well as the native British tradition of sceptical empiricism to which Bradley was an heir. Most controversial of all, there is the question of the influence of Hegel. Was Bradley, or was he not, a Hegelian? Similar disagreements occur about whom he was directing his philosophy against. While some see his chief targets as the British schools of empiricism and utilitarianism, originating in Mill,[3] he has also been portrayed as a critic of the Hegelians and Kantians.[4]

Moving to more substantial issues, there is disagreement about the relative roles of logic and metaphysics in his philosophy. Was he primarily a logician or a metaphysician? While some have regarded him at bottom as a metaphysician, and only consequently as an advocate of something sometimes called 'idealist logic', others have tried to separate his logic from, and emphasize it over, his metaphysics.[5] There is similar disagreement about whether to

---

[1] Stirling (1865); Green (1885–8); Caird (1893).
[2] Lotze (1884); Herbart (1850–93), i; Sigwart (1895); Wundt (1897).
[3] Wollheim (1969); McHenry (1992).   [4] Muirhead (1931), 219.
[5] Contrast Vander Veer (1970) and Manser (1983).

classify him as an advocate of empiricism or of rationalism. On the one hand, Russell saw him as a member of what he called 'the classical tradition' in philosophy, which he characterized as holding the belief that one can discover otherwise unknowable secrets about the universe through purely a priori reasoning, whilst being immune to empirical criticisms. On the other hand, in his papers, Cresswell sees Bradley's position as one of extreme empiricism.[6]

It should also be clear that the list given is no mere set of disconnected interpretative disputes. While there is no necessity for an answer to one question to determine the answer to another, there is a clear affinity between certain of these different interpretations. In general, we might say that those who interpret Bradley tend to fall into one of two camps. There are those who place him in the Hegelian rationalist tradition and those (fewer) who see him as a direct descendant of the British empiricists. These differences perhaps come out most clearly in the different philosophers with whom he is compared or said to have affinities. It is common to compare him with other monists and idealists—with, for instance, Spinoza, Hegel, and Bosanquet (it has even been said that Bradley's philosophy is so close to Bosanquet's that we had better think of them as a single philosopher[7]), or even those Indian philosophers of the Vedantic tradition.[8] But others have noted quite different similarities—for instance, with Frege, Russell, Wittgenstein, and Quine.[9]

It has been my position in this book that no such partisan divisions can do justice either to the complex subtlety or the originality of Bradley's thought. The truth of the matter is that he combines both of these strands into a single system. We have seen, for instance, that both his influences and targets were numerous and diverse, and in particular we have discussed at length his complex relationship to Hegel, noting that it is simultaneously one of great debt and deep opposition. It has also been noted that, for Bradley, neither logic nor metaphysics can be given supremacy, but rather that they need to be viewed as mutually supporting and entailing aspects of a single intellectual enterprise. And we have

---

[6] Contrast Russell ((1914), 5) and Cresswell (1977; 1979).
[7] Mackenzie (1928), 235. But, for more thoughtful positions, see Cuming (1917) and Robinson (1980).   [8] Shrivastava (1968).
[9] Ryle (1956); Passmore (1969); Manser (1984); Manser and Stock (1984); Stock (1985).

seen also how he combines a deep empiricism with a firm faith in inference from logical principles. The net result, as we have observed, is that his thought may be fruitfully compared with a large number of very different philosophers. The whole truth is not to be found on either side. In order to re-present and strengthen that result let us look at another combination within, and consequent disagreement between critics about, his philosophy.

8.2 CAUTION AND CONSTRUCTION

It has been remarked more than once[10] that Bradley's philosophy contains an unusual combination of cautious scepticism about the faculty of human thought and courageous system-building in the grand style. Initial evidence of this combination of scepticism and system-building is not hard to find.

On the one hand, we may consider the numerous self-effacing remarks with which he prefaced all of his major books. His *Principles of Logic*, he says, 'makes no claim to supply any systematic treatment of Logic' (*PL*, p. ix). Later in the same Preface, in rejecting the charge of being a Hegelian, he significantly says,

What interests me is something very different. We want no system-making or systems home-grown or imported. . . . What we want at present is to clear the ground, so that English Philosophy, if it rises, may not be choked by prejudice. The ground can not be cleared without a critical, or, if you prefer it, a sceptical study of first principles. (*PL*, p. x)

In the same mood, he describes *Appearance and Reality* as merely an 'essay' in metaphysics, for 'Neither in form nor extent does it carry out the idea of a system' (*AR*, p. vii). A little later he adds, 'My book does not design to be permanent, and will be satisfied to be negative, so long as that word implies an attitude of active questioning. The chief need of English philosophy is, I think, a sceptical study of first principles' (*AR*, p. viii).

On the other hand, these statements do not sit easily with the content of those works. If system-building is the construction of complex and all-encompassing theories of the nature and structure of reality, which go beyond what is immediately observed, then

---

[10] Campbell (1931); Copleston (1966), 187; Wollheim (1969), 17; Candlish (1984); McHenry (1992), 14.

his philosophy is full of system-building. What is his theory of the Absolute but a metaphysical system? He himself describes metaphysics as 'the effort to comprehend the universe, not simply piecemeal or by fragments, but somehow as a whole' (*AR* 1).

There is at least an initial or superficial tension between these two aspects of his philosophy. They do not seem to sit easily together. Many interpreters have found this an awkward conjunction, and thus tended to emphasize one or the other. On the one hand, there are those who tend to emphasize the critical or sceptical flavour of his thought. Campbell describes his work as issuing in scepticism,[11] while Wollheim, in a memorable analogy, describes him as 'like a man, forced backwards, step by step, down a strange labyrinth, in self-defence, until at last finding himself in the comparative safety of some murky cave he rests among the shadows'.[12] On the other hand, there have been those, such as Russell,[13] who have tended to see him as a classical system-builder of the worst kind.

I shall argue that both sides are wrong, that a true account of his philosophy must make room for both aspects, and should not emphasize one at the expense of excluding or diminishing the other. In order to make good this claim we need first to bring out more clearly and in greater detail these two aspects of his philosophy. This may be done by comparing his philosophy with that of an acknowledged sceptic and system-builder respectively. For this purpose let us take the figures of Hegel and Hume (at least at they are standardly interpreted).

For Hegel,[14] the Real is the rational. This allows him to work out the nature and functioning of thought and then confidently to ascribe the same structure to reality. His confidence in the power of pure thought to take us beyond the contingencies of how things may at any stage appear to how things are in themselves leads him to develop a complex architechtonic of reality as a whole.

Despite Bradley's attempts to dissociate himself from Hegel, many of the same Hegelian system-building tendencies are to be found in Bradley's own thought. If a philosophical system is a large conceptual structure built up from a slender basis and capable of explaining everything, then a philosophical system, or at

---

[11] Campbell (1931), preface.   [12] Wollheim (1969), 18.
[13] Russell (1914), 4–10.   [14] Hegel (1977).

least the framework of one, is certainly what we find in Bradley. Bradley's denials of this charge amount solely to the fact that he does not believe himself to have yet provided the necessary detail, requisite in his eyes, to justify that title. He says, 'To show how the world, physical and spiritual, realizes by various stages and degrees the one absolute principle, would involve a system of metaphysics. And such a system I am not undertaking to construct. I am endeavouring merely to get a sound general view of Reality' (*AR* 318). Yet, like Hegel, he offers a single unified account of both thought and reality, capable, in principle at least, of locating everything in the universe and placing it on a determinate scale of value. Bradley says,

We have an idea of perfection or of individuality; and, as we find that any form of existence more completely realizes this idea, we assign to it its position in the scale of being. And in this scale (as we have seen) the lower, as its defects are made good, passes beyond itself into the higher. The end, or the absolute individuality, is also the principle. Present from the first it supplies the test of its inferior stages, and, as these are included in fuller wholes, the principle grows in reality. (*AR* 440)

Also, like Hegel, he has a confidence in the compelling power of purely logical reasoning, and takes a unified theoretical approach employing a small number of critical tools to all problems, no matter how diverse. This is quite different from the small scale, fragmentary, and multi-methoded approach typical of modern analytic philosophy. Moreover, in so far as Bradley's Absolute is something transcending even thought itself, Bradley might be thought of as a bolder system-builder than Hegel.

Turning from system-building to scepticism, let us consider the figure of Hume.[15] Where Hegel emphasizes Logic, Hume stresses actual experience as it is in fact presented to us. Moreover, he doubts that we have any good reason to believe that the forms of thought match up in any significant way with reality. This scepticism that any way we might choose to extend our knowledge should match up with reality itself leads to a complex descriptive methodology.

While there are significant differences between Bradley and Hume (Hume's atomism, for instance, is in sharp variance with Bradley's holism), the similarities between them are far greater than has

[15] Hume (1975).

usually been noticed. Both, for instance, place a strong emphasis on the deliverances of immediate experience as the only legitimate source of knowledge. But more germane to our purpose here, Hume's writings are predominantly sceptical in tone and result, and, as we have seen in the prefaces to his own books, Bradley explicitly attributes the same character to his own work. Nor are these self-effacing remarks a dishonest modesty, for he does share Hume's fundamental scepticism about our claims to, and even our ability to arrive at, knowledge of how things really are. One by one the most fundamental concepts and categories that we use to order and classify experience are criticized as deficient or false. If anything, concerning the relation between thought and reality, Bradley is a more trenchant sceptic than Hume. Where Hume sees no good reason for believing that they coincide, Bradley makes a positive and certain denial that they ever can or do. Thus in some respects he is more of a sceptic than Hume.

It would be hard to find two figures more philosophically opposed than Hegel and Hume. Yet Bradley's system has deep affinities with both of them. How is this achieved? We already have, in the previous chapters, the necessary material to see how this is done. But let us spell out the point. Bradley's solution can be most clearly seen by concentrating on the principal difference between Hegel and Hume. One asserts, while the other denies, the identity of thought and reality. Bradley has sympathy with both these positions and reconciles them by replacing the relation of identity with the relation of a part to its whole. The same point could be put in another way. Hegel is a monist and Hume a dualist. Bradley reconciles the positions by setting up a Humean dualism within the Hegelian monism.

The way in which we have presented this reconciliation so far is rather abstract and formal, and might suggest a rather arbitrary union of ultimately incongruous elements. Against this, it needs to be shown how in Bradley's philosophy these two elements are neatly dovetailed together into a harmonious whole. Although there remains room in the end to doubt the ultimate success of the union, it cannot simply be dismissed from the outset as lacking serious foundation. In order to demonstrate this I shall attempt to draw out two things: first, that his system-building grows out of his scepticism, and, secondly, that his scepticism depends on his system-building.

Bradley's system-building tendencies are most fully realized in his notion of the all-encompassing Absolute. Yet the existence, nature, and mode of presentation of this Absolute are all direct consequences of, and inseparable from, his deep-rooted scepticism. This scepticism consists primarily in the fact that he is unable to accept the basic Hegelian identity between thought and reality. 'I could not accept what seems his main principle, or at least part of that principle' (*PL*, p. x), he explains, for he is 'unable to verify a solution of this kind' (*AR* 507). The direct consequence of this scepticism is that there must exist a reality which is more than just thought. This is interesting, for scepticism is usually thought to have metaphysically deflationary consequences. Here, however, through doubting one of the more radical claims of Hegelian metaphysics, Bradley yields a strongly realist conclusion.

Moreover, his critical or sceptical approach to the categories of thought also determines the precise nature of that conclusion. The forms of thought are held to be contradictory because they are relational; however, this critique itself determines the nature of reality, for it implies the existence of a touchstone or standard, which, although not met here in this particular case, must be met by anything deserving the status of reality.

Even the mode of presenting this reality may be seen as a function of Bradley's scepticism. Since all thought fails these standards, the Absolute cannot be given in thought. However, by locating the flaws of thought, Bradley is also able to say what would be necessary to rectify them. It is by following this path that we arrive at the nature of the Absolute. Thus the Absolute is not specified positively or directly, but negatively and indirectly as the limit of the process of correcting the flaws and inconsistencies of thought. Thus all that we know of the metaphysics of the Absolute derives from Bradley's searching and sceptical criticism of the tools of thought.

But, on the other hand, just as much as Bradley's metaphysics derives from his scepticism, his scepticism might be said to derive from his metaphysics, for it is his conception of the Absolute which necessitates his scepticism. This may be seen in at least two places. First, he has a firm and basic conviction that those aspects of life which neither consist in thought, nor can be reduced to it, none the less have an important place in ultimate reality. That is what leads him to postulate both an immediate experience and a final Absolute whose fundamental nature consists, not in thought, but in feeling or experience. This emphasis on feeling grounds his hostility to the identity of thought and reality, and his consequent scepticism about the ability of thought to determine the complete nature of ultimate reality.

A second example of how the Absolute necessarily engenders scepticism can be seen in the foundations of his logic. Bradley's firm faith in the nature of ultimate reality finds expression in what he takes to be the fundamental laws of logic and criticism. These are the critical tools which drive the sceptical machine and before which everything must fall. But the absolute faith he has in the laws of identity and non-contradiction is based wholly upon his firm belief that these are the only possible laws of reality. They are the metaphysical axioms of his scepticism.

Scepticism then derives from metaphysics no less than metaphysics derives from scepticism. This might be thought to be circular. But Bradley would view this dual relationship as but two sides of a single coin. This is not a kind of bootstrapping situation where each is to be cited as support for the other. The case is rather (as in the relationship between logic and metaphysics) that, by mutually supporting and entailing each other, they achieve together what neither is capable of achieving on its own. Nor in the end is this combination so strange. Total scepticism is self-defeating, but, if we are to avoid the other extreme of dogmatism, the only answer is to hold something firm (at least for the moment), while we criticize everything else. And is this not the method of all critical philosophy? Of course, how much is held firm or criticized and how strongly or confidently this is done vary from philosopher to philosopher. There is a range of positions. What makes Bradley's thought so distinctive is that he lies near one end of this range. He combines extreme confidence in a very small number of axioms, with a merciless critique of the very large field that remains.

8.3 CONCLUSION

We have attempted to demonstrate just how Bradley's philosophy reconciles sceptical epistemology and constructive metaphysics, and thus to argue that it is an interpretative mistake to try to force his thought into one mould or the other. But in doing this we have also strengthened our case for claiming that the same holds for the other disagreements also. Just as with the case of construction and scepticism, the pairs that are held in opposition are really an integral whole within Bradley's thought.

The history of Bradley scholarship is not exemplary. In far too many cases the basic approach has been wrong, for all too often the name of the game has been fame or infamy by association. This was certainly evident among his contemporaries. Russell indulged in attacking Bradley by associating him with the name of Hegel, rather than engaging him directly; he is often critical or dismissive of those whom he calls Hegelians or idealists, where it is quite clear from the context that his primary target is Bradley (and perhaps to a lesser extent McTaggart).[16] Yet other Hegelians, like Bosanquet,[17] tended simply to assimilate Bradley to their own position, or at least to down-play the significance of any unorthodox wanderings from the fold of Hegelian truth. Very sensibly, Bradley himself favoured dropping the whole question, and said of Hegel, 'I have no wish to conceal how much I owe to his writings; but I will leave it to those who can judge better than myself, to fix the limits within which I have followed him' (*PL*, p. x). Meanwhile the pragmatists tried to assimilate him to their own position. For instance, one of their number, F. C. S. Schiller, wrote a long series of largely worthless papers over many years claiming that Bradley's position was in effect the same as his own.[18]

Russell's camp, of course, won the day. But the debate does not stop there. Many recent philosophers, by attributing a coherence theory of truth to Bradley, have thought that they can thereby assimilate him to the anti-realist fold.[19] But this, as we have seen, is to mistake his actual view of truth, and also to ignore his strong realist sympathies. In a different vein, Cresswell's attempt[20] to present Bradley as an extreme empiricist was, rather mischievously, but not I think inaccurately, described by Candlish as implying that

---

[16] Russell (1914), 4–10; (1927), 262–4; (1956a), 245; (1967), 83–4.

[17] Bosanquet (1911).

[18] Schiller (1903; 1907; 1908; 1910a; 1910b; 1913; 1915; 1917; 1925).

[19] Grayling (1982), 281; Manser (1983); Blackburn (1984); Dancy (1985), 137–8.   [20] Cresswell (1977; 1979).

The rumours of a foreign paternity for Bradley's metaphysics are thus to be dismissed, presumably, as mere malicious Cambridge gossip, motivated perhaps by a desire to usurp Bradley's place as the legitimate claimant of the respect due to the British Empiricists' descendants.[21]

Thus the parties quarrel over his suitability for membership of their ranks alternately as though he were a rich benefactor or a leper. The point of this game is whether or not (by their own standards) to take him seriously. But my claim is that, even when they seek his association, by this game, both sides in fact belittle and underestimate him. I hope to have shown that he combines in his thought many different ideas and affinities, and this is why he should be taken seriously. His philosophy is a unique combination of empiricism and rationalism, and cannot be understood by emphasizing one element at the expense of the other. He stands with one foot squarely in each camp, and thus, unlike perhaps Green or Bosanquet, is one philosopher of his group, for who the term 'Anglo-Hegelian' truly describes his philosophy. It is precisely this unique combination that makes his philosophy interesting and, so long as there exists a division between empiricist and rationalist traditions of thought, well worth the study of any serious student of philosophy.

[21] Candlish (1981), 242.

REFERENCES

THE most up to date and complete bibliography of works by and on Bradley is R. Ingardia (1991), *Bradley: A Research Bibliography* (Bowling Green, Ohio: Philosophical Documentation Center).

Acton, H. B. (1967), 'Bradley, Francis Herbert', in P. Edwards (ed.), *The Encyclopedia of Philosophy* (London: Collier-Macmillan), i. 359–63.

Airaksinen, T. (1975), *The Ontological Criteria of Reality* (Turku: Turun Yliopisto).

Alexander, H. G. (1956) (ed.), *The Leibniz–Clarke Correspondence* (Manchester: Manchester University Press).

Allard, J. (1984), 'Bradley's Principle of Sufficient Reason', in A. Manser and G. Stock (eds.), *The Philosophy of F. H. Bradley* (Oxford: Clarendon Press), 173–89.

—— (1985), 'Bradley's Intensional Judgements', *History of Philosophy Quarterly*, 2: 469–75.

—— (1986), 'Wollheim on Bradley on Subjects and Predicates', *Idealistic Studies*, 16: 27–40.

—— (1989), 'Bradley on the Validity of Inference', *Journal of the History of Philosophy*, 27: 267–84.

Augustine (1961), *Confessions*, trans. R. S. Pine-Coffin (Harmondsworth: Penguin Books).

Ayer, A. J. (1935), 'Internal Relations', *Proceedings of the Aristotelian Society*, suppl. vol. 14: 173–85.

—— (1952), 'Negation', *Journal of Philosophy*, 49: 797–815.

Baldwin, T. (1991), 'The Identity Theory of Truth', *Mind*, 100: 35–52.

Bedell, G. L. (1971), 'The Relation of Logic and Metaphysics in the Philosophy of F. H. Bradley', *Modern Schoolman*, 48: 221–35.

—— (1977), 'Bradley and Hegel', *Idealistic Studies*, 7: 262–90.

Bell, D. (1984), 'The Insufficiency of Ethics', in A. Manser and G. Stock (eds.), *The Philosophy of F. H. Bradley* (Oxford: Clarendon Press), 53–76.

Bergson, H. (1911), *Creative Evolution*, trans. A. Mitchell (London: Macmillan and Co.).

Berkeley, G. (1944), *Philosophical Commentaries*, ed. A. A. Luce (Edinburgh: Thomas Nelson).

Berkeley, G. (1948–57), *The Principles of Human Knowledge*, in *The Works of George Berkeley*, ed. A. A. Luce and T. E. Jessop (Edinburgh: Thomas Nelson), ii. 19–113.

Blackburn, S. (1984), 'Is Epistemology Incoherent?', in A. Manser and G. Stock (eds.), *The Philosophy of F. H. Bradley* (Oxford: Clarendon Press), 155–73.

Blanshard, B. (1984), 'Bradley on Relations', in A. Manser and G. Stock (eds.), *The Philosophy of F. H. Bradley* (Oxford: Clarendon Press), 211–26.

Bosanquet, B. (1885*a*), 'Mr. F. H. Bradley on Fact and Inference', *Mind*, OS 10: 256–65.

—— (1885*b*), *Knowledge and Reality* (London: Kegan Paul, Trench and Co.).

—— (1911), *Logic, or The Morphology of Knowledge*, 2nd edn. (Oxford: Clarendon Press).

Bradley, J. (1984), 'F. H. Bradley's Metaphysics of Feeling and its Place in the History of Philosophy', in A. Manser and G. Stock (eds.), *The Philosophy of F. H. Bradley* (Oxford: Clarendon Press), 227–42.

Broad, C. D. (1933), *An Examination of McTaggart's Philosophy* (Cambridge: Cambridge University Press), i.

Caird, E. (1893), *Hegel* (London: William Blackwood and Sons).

Campbell, C. A. (1931), *Scepticism and Construction, Bradley's Sceptical Principle as the Basis of Constructive Philosophy* (London: George Allen and Unwin).

Candlish, S. (1978), 'Bradley on My Station and its Duties', *Australasian Journal of Philosophy*, 56: 155–70.

—— (1981), 'The Status of Idealism in Bradley's Metaphysics', *Idealistic Studies*, 11: 242–53.

—— (1982), 'Idealism and Bradley's Logic', *Idealistic Studies*, 12: 251–9.

—— (1984), 'Scepticism, Ideal Experiment, and Priorities in Bradley's Metaphysics', in A. Manser and G. Stock (eds.), *The Philosophy of F. H. Bradley* (Oxford: Clarendon Press), 243–67.

—— (1989), 'The Truth about F. H. Bradley', *Mind*, 98: 331–48.

Church, R. W. (1942*a*), *Bradley's Dialectic* (London: George Allen and Unwin).

—— (1942*b*), 'Bradley's Theory of Relations and the Law of Identity', *Philosophical Review*, 51: 26–46.

Cook Wilson, J. (1926), *Statement and Inference* (Oxford: Clarendon Press).

Copleston, F. (1966), *A History of Philosophy* (London: Burns and Oates Ltd.), viii.

Cresswell, M. J. (1977), 'Reality as Experience in F. H. Bradley', *Australasian Journal of Philosophy*, 55: 169–88.

—— (1979), 'Bradley's Theory of Judgement', *Canadian Journal of Philosophy*, 9: 575–94.

Cuming, A. (1917), 'Lotze, Bradley and Bosanquet', *Mind*, 26: 162–70.

Dancy, J. (1985), *Introduction to Contemporary Epistemology* (Oxford: Basil Blackwell).

Dawes Hicks, G. (1925), 'Mr. Bradley's Treatment of Nature', *Mind*, 34: 55–69.

Delany, C. F. (1971), 'Bradley on the Nature of Science', *Idealistic Studies*, 1: 201–18.

Descartes, R. (1911), 'Meditations on First Philosophy', trans. E. S. Haldane and G. R. T. Ross, in *The Philosophical Works of Descartes* (Cambridge: Cambridge University Press).

Eliot, T. S. (1975), 'Francis Herbert Bradley', in his *Selected Prose*, ed. F. Kermode (London: Faber and Faber), 196–204.

Ewing, A. C. (1934), *Idealism: A Critical Survey* (London: Methuen and Co. Ltd.).

Findlay, J. N. (1958), *Hegel: A Re-Examination* (London: George Allen and Unwin).

Foster, M. B. (1930), 'The Contradiction of "Appearance and Reality"', *Mind*, 39: 43–60.

Frege, G. (1980), *Translations from the Philosophical Writings of Gottlob Frege*, ed. P. Geach and M. Black, 3rd edn. (Oxford: Basil Blackwell).

Grayling, A. (1982), *An Introduction to Philosophical Logic* (Brighton: Harvester Press).

Green, T. H. (1885–8), *Works* (3 vols.; London: Longmans, Green and Co.).

Griffin, N. (1983), 'What's Wrong with Bradley's Theory of Judgement?', *Idealistic Studies*, 13: 199–225.

Grünbaum, A. (1973), *Philosophical Problems of Space and Time*, 2nd edn. (Dordrecht: D. Reidel).

Haack, S. (1978), *Philosophy of Logics* (Cambridge: Cambridge University Press).

Hegel, G. W. F. (1929), *Hegel's Science of Logic*, trans. W. H. Johnston and L. G. Struthers (2 vols.; London: George Allen and Unwin Ltd.).

—— (1975), *Hegel's Logic*, trans. W. Wallace, 3rd edn. (Oxford: Clarendon Press).

—— (1977), *The Phenomenology of Spirit*, trans. A. V. Miller (Oxford: Clarendon Press).

Herbart, J. F. (1850–93), *Sämtliche Werke*, ed. G. Hartenstein (13 vols.; Leipzig: Verlag von Leopold Voss).

Hume, D. (1975), *Enquiries Concerning Human Understanding and Concerning the Principles of Morals*, ed. L. A. Selby-Bigge, 3rd edn. (Oxford: Clarendon Press).

Hylton, P. (1990), *Russell, Idealism and the Emergence of Analytic Philosophy* (Oxford: Clarendon Press).

James, W. (1893a), 'Mr. Bradley on Immediate Resemblance', *Mind*, 2: 208–10.

—— (1893b), 'Immediate Resemblance', *Mind*, 2: 509–10.

—— (1907), *Pragmatism, a New Name for Some Old Ways of Thinking* (London: Longmans, Green and Co.).

—— (1910), 'Bradley or Bergson?', *Journal of Philosophy*, 7: 29–33.

Jevons, W. S. (1879), *The Principles of Science*, 3rd edn. (London: Macmillan and Co.).

Joachim, H. H. (1906), *The Nature of Truth* (Oxford: Clarendon Press).

Johnson, P. (1984), 'Bradley and the Nature of Punishment', in A. Manser and G. Stock (eds.), *The Philosophy of F. H. Bradley* (Oxford: Clarendon Press), 99–116.

Kagey, R. (1931*a*), *The Growth of F. H. Bradley's Logic* (London: Macmillan).

—— (1931*b*), 'Review: *Appearance and Reality*', *Journal of Philosophy*, 28: 137–9.

Kant, I. (1929), *The Critique of Pure Reason*, trans. N. Kemp Smith (London: Macmillan Press Ltd.).

Keen, C. N. (1971), 'The Interaction of Russell and Bradley', *Russell: The Journal of the Bertrand Russell Archives*, 3: 7–11.

Kenna, J. C. (1966), 'Ten Unpublished Letters from William James, 1842–1910, to Francis Herbert Bradley, 1846–1924', *Mind*, 75: 309–31.

Kripke, S. (1980), *Naming and Necessity* (Oxford: Basil Blackwell).

Kulkarni, N. G. (1957), 'Bradley's Anti-Relational Argument', *Philosophical Quarterly*, 7: 97–108.

Lotze, H. (1884), *System of Philosophy*, ed. B. Bosanquet (2 vols.; Oxford: Clarendon Press).

Mack, R. D. (1945), *The Appeal to Immediate Experience, Philosophic Method in Bradley, Whitehead and Dewey* (New York: King and Crown Press).

Mackenzie, J. S. (1894), 'Mr. Bradley's View of the Self', *Mind*, 3: 304–35.

—— (1928), 'Review: *Ethical Studies*', *Mind*, 37: 233–8.

Maclachlan, D. L. C. (1963), 'Presupposition in Bradley's Philosophy', *Dialogue*, 2: 155–69.

Mander, W. J. (1991), 'F. H. Bradley and the Philosophy of Science', *International Studies in the Philosophy of Science*, 5: 65–78.

Manser, A. (1983), *Bradley's Logic* (Oxford: Basil Blackwell).

—— (1984), 'Bradley and Frege', in A. Manser and G. Stock (eds.), *The Philosophy of F. H. Bradley* (Oxford: Clarendon Press), 303–17.

—— Stock, G. (1984), 'Introduction', in A. Manser and G. Stock (eds.), *The Philosophy of F. H. Bradley* (Oxford: Clarendon Press), 1–32.

Martin, R. M. (1977), 'On Peirce, Bradley and the Doctrine of Continuous Relations', *Idealistic Studies*, 7: 291–304.

McHenry, L. B. (1992), *Whitehead and Bradley: A Comparative Analysis* (Albany: State University of New York Press).

Mill, J. S. (1872), *A System of Logic*, 8th edn. (London: Longmans, Green and Co.).

Montague, R. (1964), 'Wollheim on Bradley on Idealism and Relations', *Philosophical Quarterly*, 14: 158–64.

Moore, G. E. (1922*a*), 'The Conception of Reality', in his *Philosophical Studies* (London: Kegan Paul, Trench and Trubner), 197–219.

—— (1922*b*), 'External and Internal Relations', in his *Philosophical Studies* (London: Kegan Paul, Trench and Trubner), 276–309.

Muirhead, J. H. (1931), *The Platonic Tradition in Anglo-Saxon Philosophy* (London: George Allen and Unwin).

Mure, G. R. G. (1961), 'F. H. Bradley—Towards a Portrait', *Encounter*, 16: 28–35.

Newton-Smith, W. H. (1980), *The Structure of Time* (London: Routledge and Kegan Paul).

Nicholson, P. P. (1990), *The Political Philosophy of the British Idealists* (Cambridge: Cambridge University Press).

Passmore, J. (1966), *A Hundred years of Philosophy*, 2nd edn. (Harmondsworth: Penguin Books).

—— (1969), 'Russell and Bradley', in R. Brown and C. D. Rollins (eds.), *Contemporary Philosophy in Australia* (London: George Allen and Unwin), 21–30.

—— (1976), 'G. F. Stout's Editorship of *Mind* (1892–1920)', *Mind*, 85: 17–36.

Pattison, M. (1876), 'Philosophy at Oxford', *Mind*, os 1: 82–97.

Pears, D. F. (1967), *Bertrand Russell and the British Tradition in Philosophy* (London: Fontana).

Peirce, C. S. (1955), 'The Fixation of Belief', in his *Philosophical Writings of Peirce*, ed. J. Buchler (New York: Dover Publications).

Pringle Pattison, A. S. (1902), 'A New Theory of the Absolute', in his *Man's Place in the Cosmos*, 2nd edn. (London: William Blackwood and Sons), 92–158.

Putnam, H. (1981), *Reason, Truth and History* (Cambridge: Cambridge University Press).

Robinson, J. (1980), 'Bradley and Bosanquet', *Idealistic Studies*, 10: 1–23.

Russell, B. (1903), *The Principles of Mathematics* (London: George Allen and Unwin).

—— (1906–7), 'On the Nature of Truth', *Proceedings of the Aristotelian Society*, 7: 28–49.

—— (1910), 'Some Explanations in Reply to Mr. Bradley', *Mind*, 19: 373–8.

—— (1910–11), 'Knowledge by Acquaintance and Knowledge by Description', *Proceedings of the Aristotelian Society*, 11: 108–28.

—— (1914), *Our Knowledge of the External World* (London: Open Court Publishing).

—— (1927), *An Outline of Philosophy* (London: George Allen and Unwin).

—— (1956*a*), 'The Philosophy of Logical Atomism', in his *Logic and Knowledge*, ed. R. C. Marsh (London: George Allen and Unwin), 177–281.

—— (1956*b*), 'Logical Atomism', in his *Logic and Knowledge,* ed. R. C. Marsh (London: George Allen and Unwin), 323–43.

—— (1959), *My Philosophical Development* (London: George Allen and Unwin).

—— (1967), *The Problems of Philosophy* (Oxford: Oxford University Press Paperbacks).

—— (1975), *Autobiography* (London: Unwin Paperbacks).

—— (1989), *Wisdom of the West,* ed. P. Foulkes (London: Bloomsbury Books).

Ryle, G. (1956), 'Introduction', in A. J. Ayer *et al.* (eds.), *The Revolution in Philosophy* (London: Macmillan and Co. Ltd.), 1–11.

Saxena, S. K. (1967), *Studies in the Metaphysics of Bradley* (London: George Allen and Unwin).

Schiller, F. C. S. (1903), 'On Preserving Appearances', *Mind,* 12: 341–54.

—— (1907), 'Mr. Bradley's Theory of Truth', *Mind,* 16: 401–9.

—— (1908), 'Is Mr. Bradley becoming a Pragmatist?', *Mind,* 17: 370–83.

—— (1910*a*), 'The Present Phase of "Idealist" Philosophy', *Mind,* 19: 30–45.

—— (1910*b*), 'Absolutism *in Extremis?*', *Mind,* 19: 533–40.

—— (1913), 'Mysticism v. Intellectualism', *Mind,* 22: 87–9.

—— (1915), 'The New Developments of Mr. Bradley's Philosophy', *Mind,* 24: 345–66.

—— (1917), 'Mr. Bradley, Bain and Pragmatism', *Journal of Philosophy,* 14: 449–57.

—— (1925), 'The Origin of Bradley's Scepticism', *Mind,* 34: 217–33.

Schopenhauer, A. (1969), *The World as Will and Representation,* trans. E. F. J. Payne (New York: Dover Publications).

Segerstedt, T. T. (1934), *Value and Reality in Bradley's Philosophy* (Lund: A–B Gleerupska Univ. Bookhandeln).

Shrivastava, S. N. L. (1968), *Samkara and Bradley* (Delhi: Motilal Banarsidass).

Sidgwick, A. (1894), 'Mr. Bradley and the Sceptics', *Mind,* 3: 336–47.

—— (1904), 'On a Note of Mr. Bradley's', *Mind,* 13: 592.

—— (1905), 'Mr. Bradley's Dilemma', *Mind,* 14: 293–4.

—— (1908), 'The Ambiguity of Pragmatism', *Mind,* 17: 368–9.

—— (1909), 'Notes on a Note', *Mind,* 18: 639–40.

Sigwart, C. (1895), *Logic,* trans. H. Dendy (London: Swan Sonnenschein).

Silkstone, T. W. (1974), 'Bradley on Relations', *Idealistic Studies,* 4: 160–9.

Sprigge, T. (1979), 'Russell and Bradley on Relations', in G. Roberts (ed.), *Bertrand Russell Memorial Volume* (London: George Allen and Unwin), 150–70.

—— (1983), *The Vindication of Absolute Idealism* (Edinburgh: University of Edinburgh Press).

Stirling, J. H. (1865), *The Secret of Hegel* (London: Longmans).

Stock, G. (1985), 'Negation: Bradley and Wittgenstein', *Philosophy*, 60: 465–76.

Swabey, W. C. (1919), 'Bradley's Negative Dialectic and Realism', *Journal of Philosophy*, 16: 404–17.

Taylor, A. E. (1924–5), 'Francis Herbert Bradley', *Proceedings of the British Academy*, 11: 458–68.

—— (1925), 'F. H. Bradley', *Mind*, 34: 1–12.

—— (1937), 'Bradley, Francis Herbert', in J. H. R. Weaver (ed.), *Dictionary of National Biography*, 1922–30 (London: Oxford University Press), 101–3.

Vander Veer, G. L. (1970), *Bradley's Metaphysics and the Self* (London: Yale University Press).

Walsh, W. H. (1964), 'F. H. Bradley', in D. J. O'Connor (ed.), A *Critical History of Western Philosophy* (Basingstoke: Macmillan).

Ward, J. (1894), 'Critical Notice: *Appearance and Reality*', *Mind*, 3: 109–25.

Whitehead, A. N. (1929), *Process and Reality* (New York: Macmillan Company).

Wittgenstein, L. (1961), *Tractatus logico-philosophicus*, trans. D. F. Pears and B. F. McGuinness (London: Routledge and Kegan Paul).

Wollheim, R. (1969), *F. H. Bradley*, 2nd edn. (Harmondsworth: Penguin Books).

—— (1970), 'Eliot and F. H. Bradley; An Account', in G. Martin (ed.), *Eliot in Perspective: A Symposium* (London: Macmillan), 169–93.

Wright, C. (1984), 'The Moral Organism', in A. Manser and G. Stock (eds.), *The Philosophy of F. H. Bradley* (Oxford: Clarendon Press), 77–97.

Wundt, W. (1897), *Outlines of Psychology*, trans. C. H. Judd (Leipzig: William Engelmann).

INDEX

absolute, the:
  appearance and 50, 136–41,
    150–5
  beyond understanding 36–7
  idealist nature of 124, 133–4
  immediate experience and 14, 73
  satisfaction and 5
abstraction 58, 86, 90, 103, 143
Acton, H. B. 150 n.
Allard, J. 51
appearance:
  Bradley's use of term 135–6
  grades of 145, 149–50
  relation to absolute 136–41,
    150–5
Augustine 122–3
Ayer, A. J. 45, 47–8, 53

Bergson, H. 12
Berkeley, G. 128–9, 132
Bosanquet, B. 16, 24, 31, 143, 157,
  164
Broad, C. D. 51, 92

Caird, E. 156
Campbell, C. A. 159
Candlish, S. 7–8, 41–2, 164–5
coherence and comprehensiveness
  38–9
contraiety and contradiction 4, 26,
  38, 44, 46–8, 49–55
Cook Wilson, J. 93
Copleston, F. 158
Cresswell, M. J. 11 n., 14, 124–5,
  157, 164

definite description 74–5
demonstratives 72–4
Descartes, R. 9, 15, 31

Eliot, T. S. 2, 135 n.
empiricism 2, 10, 13–14, 39, 157,
  164–5
ethics 5, 36
existence and content 12, 32, 33, 36,
  66, 142

facts:
  bare facts 13–14, 39–41
  negative facts 45–6
Foster, M. B. 137, 150 n., 153
foundationalism 15–16, 27, 44, 51
Frege, G. 61, 66

geometry 119–20
Green, T. H. 2, 156
Grünbaum, A. 117

Hegel, G. W. F.:
  abstract identity 48
  Bradley's critique of 9, 14, 25, 26,
    31, 32, 36–7, 57–8
  on demonstratives 72
  dialectic 19, 54
  formal logic 19, 25
  idealism 126–7
  identity-in-difference 55 n.
  introduction into England 2
  on thought and reality 9–10, 12,
    30, 57, 159–60
Hegelianism 30, 37, 55 n., 56, 157,
  165
Herbart, J. F. 2, 69–70, 156
Hume, D. 160–1

ideas:
  floating ideas 63, 143–4, 67 n.
  general and abstract 35, 40, 58,
    67, 69–75
  symbolic nature 17, 32–3, 67
ideal experiment 15, 16–19, 128
idealism:
  Bradley's arguments for 132–4
  objective 125–7
  presupposed 124–5
  relations and 132–4
  subjective 125, 127–32
identity:
  abstract identity 48–9, 55, 65, 80,
    82
  identity-in-difference 55–6, 57,
    81–2
  predication and 64–5, 79–81

indexicals, *see* demonstratives
inference 16–17, 19, 26
instinct 22–3
intellectual satisfaction 4–10, 19,
    22–3, 43
internal realism 148
intuition 51
immediate experience:
    absolute and 14, 73
    contradictory nature of 12, 14,
    39
    nature of 10–14, 35, 51
    non-relational 11, 87
    reality and 10–11, 31, 33, 39

James, W. 8, 12, 42
Jevons, W. S. 64–5
Joachim, H. H. 37
judgement:
    Bradley's theory of 26, 33–6, 60,
    68, 141–5
    hypothetical judgement 17–69
    logical form 61–2
    proposition and 28–9, 59, 62–3,
    143
    subject–predicate 59–76, 136

Kant, I. 2, 21, 40, 112–13, 139–40
Kripke, S. 71–2
Kulkani, N. G. 56

Leibniz, G. W. F. 112, 116
logic:
    formal logic 7, 25
    metaphysics and 24–7, 44
logical empiricism 2
Lotze, H. 2, 156

Maclachlan, D. L. C. 34, 49
Manser, A. 99–100
McHenry, L. B. 108 n.
metaphysics:
    basic need for 22–3
    definition 20–3
    desire to avoid 25–6, 39, 41
    relation to logic 24–7, 44
methodology 3–20
Mill, J. S. 2, 71, 156
monism 26, 50, 56, 58–9, 84,
    109–11
Moore, G. E. 98, 136–7, 150–1
mysticism 37

names 70–2
natural science 24, 139
negation 17, 26, 45–8, 50, 51–4,
    55
    see also Ayer; Russell on negation

Pears, D. F. 101
Peirce, C. S. 8
phenomenalism 138–9
philosophy 5
pragmatism 2, 8, 42–4, 147–8,
    164
present 121–3
psychological attitude 66–7

qualities, see relations

reality:
    difference from thought 14, 25, 36,
    57–9
    feeling and 10–11, 31, 33,
    39
    identity with thought 9–10, 12, 25,
    29–37, 44
    individual nature 32, 33–4, 40
    non-contradictory 44, 50, 54
real world 144
realism 132
relations:
    asymmetrical 76
    external 101–3
    idealism and 132–4
    internal and external 96–101
    internal 103–5
    multi-place 59 n., 106
    one-place 6, 18
    qualities with 87–90
    qualities without 86–7
    unreality of 85, 94–6, 105–9
    without qualities 90–1
    with qualities 91–4
Russell, B.:
    Bradley as rationalist 95, 157, 159,
    164
    on immediate experience 51 n.
    on names 71
    on negation 45–6, 53
    objections to coherence 38–9
    predication and identity 79–80
    relations 6, 84, 90–1, 95, 109
    subject–predicate grammar 75–6,
    100–1

scepticism 19, 21–2, 158–63
Schiller, F. C. S. 42, 164
self 130–1, 135, 136
self-consciousness 9–10
Sidgwick, A. 42
Sigwart, C. 2, 156
Silkstone, T. W. 109–10
space 113–20, 136
Sprigge, T. 51, 98–9, 130
Stirling, J. H. 156
substance and adjective 77–81
sufficient reason 50–1
system-building 158–63

things in themselves 139–41
this 72–4
thisness 73
time 120–3, 136

truth:
    coherence theory of 37–9
    correspondence theory of 39–42,
        43
    degrees of truth 7, 24, 35 n., 38 n.,
        43, 141–50
    identity theory of 29–37, 38 n.,
        41–2
    pragmatic theory of 42–4

Vedanta 157

what and that, *see* existence and
        content
Whitehead, A. N. 12
Wittgenstein, L. 41, 46, 49, 71
Wollheim, R. 49, 62 n., 85, 129, 159
Wundt, W. 2, 156